WE ARE NOW CATHOLICS

Translated from the German by NORMAN C. REEVES

Edited by REV. KARL HARDT, S.J.

With an Introductory Essay by SYLVESTER P. THEISEN

THE NEWMAN PRESS • 1959 • WESTMINSTER, MARYLAND

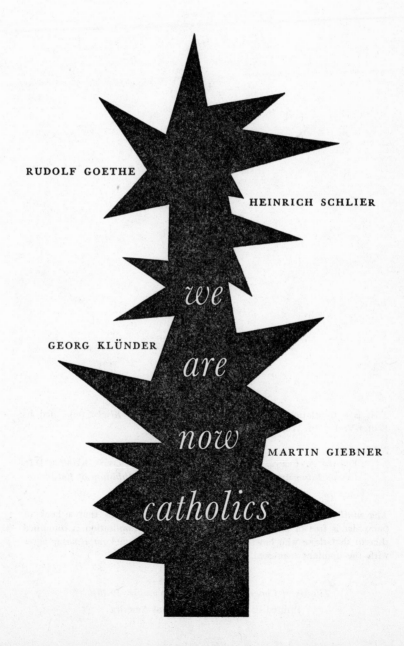

RUDOLF GOETHE

HEINRICH SCHLIER

we

GEORG KLÜNDER

are

now MARTIN GIEBNER

catholics

This is a translation of *Bekenntnis zur Katholischen Kirche* published by Echter-Verlag in Würzburg, Germany, in 1955.

Nihil obstat: *Imprimatur:*

     EDWARD A. CERNY, S.S., D.D.   FRANCIS P. KEOUGH, D.D.

     Censor Librorum   *Archbishop of Baltimore*

September 8, 1959

The *nihil obstat* and *imprimatur* are official declarations that a book or pamphlet is free of doctrinal and moral error. No implication is contained therein that those who have granted the *nihil obstat* and *imprimatur* agree with the opinions expressed.

Library of Congress Catalog Card Number: 59-10404

Printed in the United States of America

Foreword

THE WRITERS who have prepared the accounts of their conversions published in this book have joined the Catholic Church. They were all formerly Protestant theologians and practiced their ministry for many years. They occupied important positions in the Protestant Church. Pastor Giebner had been consecrated a bishop by Professor Heiler, Dr. Schlier was professor of New Testament exegesis at Bonn, Pastor Goethe was counselor to the government in the Ministry of Church Affairs in Hesse, and Dr. Klünder ministered in a parish near Berlin for eight years while pursuing his learned historical research. The fact that they had to resign their posts and give up their secure existences, indicates that they made great sacrifices for their conversion.

For all these reasons their witness to the Catholic Church is of special importance, especially as they made their decision after mature consideration and a lengthy inner struggle; for, considering their previous life, their conversion must have been both revolutionary and painful. They reached their goal by quite different routes. It would perhaps be more correct to say that they were led to the One, Holy, Catholic and Apostolic Church by the mysterious guiding star of God's grace, each from his own special field of interest. Professor Schlier was led on the "truly Protestant path" through his scientific researches in Holy Scripture; Dr. Klünder through his concern for the divine dignity of the Church and her fullness, which developed from his study of history; Pastor Giebner through his zeal for the liturgy, divine worship and the administration of the sacraments; whereas Pastor Goethe gradually prayed and lived his way into the Catholic Church.

It is the variety of the ways in which grace has led them to their goal that makes their stories so attractive and interesting.

The authority of these converts and the power of their reasonings, in combination with their experience, make their combined profession of faith a witness to the truth of the Catholic religion which is both convincing and rarely found. Their perception and reflection upon the gradual maturing of their newly-born religious insight may serve as a guide to the many who are struggling today toward belief and seeking truth. The writers would like to give to Protestants and Catholics alike a glimpse into the reasons for their conversion in order to justify their acceptance of the Catholic faith. Above all, it is felt that Catholics who read these accounts will experience more joy in their faith and a stronger loyalty, for, against the background of Protestant teaching, the value, beauty, and greatness of the Catholic faith shine forth in a completely new light. By the publication of their conversion stories, the four authors have no desire to cater to modern man's preoccupation with sensation and idle curiosity. What they want to do is to make known to all men of good will the wise providence of God and the guiding power of His grace, both of which they have experienced most profoundly in their return to the Church. By their witness to the truth, they desire to honor God and His Holy Church.

When pilgrims who have been to Rome are asked about the most striking experience of their pilgrimage, almost all reply that it is the evidence of the Church as the mother of all nations. The perception of the world-embracing unity of the Church, including as it does all nations and races, "finds its most moving expression when, in the course of a great papal audience in St. Peter's, the tens of thousands sing the Credo, the avowal of the one faith, in the one language of the Church."

The reader of these reports, too, will share to some extent in this type of experience. Each account has a distinctive character, yet all of them harmonize in their witness to the truth of the Catholic Church.

KARL HARDT, S.J.

Contents

Introductory Essay

PROTESTANT–CATHOLIC RELATIONS IN GERMANY

By Sylvester P. Theisen

THE FOUR spiritual odysseys recorded in this book are exciting stories which can be enjoyed without reading this introductory survey and without further elaboration. They are unique personal adventures. They are also, at the same time, indicative of larger religious movements in Germany today. It will, therefore, be useful to sketch the social and theological context in which these individual dramas have taken place, for a knowledge of their context will deepen the reader's appreciation of their significance.

These four German theologians have found their way from Protestantism to the Catholic Church. Those who have journeyed that far are few indeed. There are, however, many Protestants in Germany who are seriously examining their historical roots and their theological situation. Although these searchers may never be individually converted to the one true Church, they are nevertheless preparing the historical and universal dimensions for an eventual reunion of all Christians. The way to this unity is not clearly seen by them, but the exploration of possible approaches is considerably better than the complacent acceptance of the scandal of centuries, the division of Christians.

Protestants and Catholics in Germany are engaged in a theological dialogue. Americans who now hear much, thanks partly to the Fund for the Republic's seminars, about the need for a democratic dialogue between Protestants, Jews, and Catholics, will tend to think that we too have initiated such a dialogue as goes on in Germany. But there is an important difference. American discussions usually revolve around questions of power and action in our pluralistic society. Censorship, parochial schools, birth control, and other socio-moral questions are the common topics in the emerging American dialogue. With a few significant exceptions, the encounter is not on the level of worship or dogma. In Germany, on the contrary, the encounter is precisely on the level of liturgy and theology. The meaning of "faith," of "church," of "grace," of "Apostolic Succession," these are the themes that are frequently and intensely studied at meetings between Protestants and Catholics. The discussion is not about social philosophy; it is concerned with the central truths of the Christian religion. The observer is naturally led to ask the question: What factors explain the emergence of this intriguing situation in Germany?

Protestant theological trends

Martin Luther, by dethroning the Church in favor of the Bible, set in motion forces which resulted in consequences that he himself would have deplored. The Protestant principle of individual freedom of conscience in regard to the interpretation of the Bible led, along with other factors, to the development of a particular kind of pietism. This pietism made inner piety the highest religious value, independent of membership in any Church whatsoever. Religion came to depend not upon definite beliefs but only upon the psychological act of faith. Faith meant an intuitive inspiration, a living, loving impulse of the soul. The guide in religious matters was no longer the Church nor the Bible but the isolated subjective consciousness of spirituality on the part of the believers. This consciousness was naturally molded by the very personal and limited experiences of the individual Christian.

The Protestant principle of freedom of conscience was also a stimulus to the special kind of "freedom of intellect" that characterized the Enlightenment of the eighteenth century. Men no longer submitted themselves to the truths of religion and then used their reason to comprehend these truths. Instead, starting with the assumption that all things can be discovered and understood by unaided reason, they submitted the truths of religion to man's natural power of critical reasoning. After this came the influence of new theories in biology and science, such as the theory of evolutionary progress. Eventually religion was reduced to psychology and the Bible to a textbook for philology. Protestant theologians were very much involved with the contemporary intellectual currents and were greatly formed by them. Thus, by the end of the nineteenth century, various developments within German Protestant theology in the direction of naturalism had gone so far that Martin Luther, had he witnessed them, would have been painfully astonished.

Until the 1920s, Protestant theology in Germany was dominated by a kind of liberalism which is associated with the names of Ritschl (1822-1889), Harnack (1851-1930), and Hermann (1846-1922), three theologians whose influence is mentioned by several of the convert-writers in this book. Liberal theologians tried to reshape the biblical message in terms of the modern mind. They rejected special revelation, the possibility of miracles, the unique divinity of Jesus Christ, the redemption. In its place, some substituted a theology, or really a "philosophy of religion," based on immanental and evolutionary notions. For some, Christianity became nothing but an ethical doctrine. Jesus thus became merely the teacher of morality, the ideal man, the friend of the poor. Influenced by the rationalists and historicists, many Protestant theologians lost the idea of a transcendent God. In substituting reason for dogma, the natural for the supernatural, these theologians, strange as it may seem to us now, actually believed that their ideas harmonized with the spirit of Luther and the Reformation. They were, as Protestant theologians more than Catholic ones are apt to be, perfectly in tune with their own historical era, but that era did not last forever.

The First World War played an important role in the death, at least in Europe, of the liberal age, the age of shallow optimism, of naïve belief in progress, of satisfaction with naturalism. But the factor most relevant to our present discussion of theological changes was a man, the most eminent among Protestant theologians in Europe during the past few decades, the Swiss Calvinist, Karl Barth. Born in Switzerland in 1886, Barth studied in Germany under both Harnack and Hermann. His early thought therefore was in the tradition of liberal theology. But he changed very quickly, partly because the eruption of a world war made evolutionary idealism both incongruous and inadequate. In 1919 with the publication of his bulky book, *The Epistle to the Romans,* Barth's break with the liberal theological tradition was complete.

In reaction to the shallow liberals who had reduced Jesus Christ to the merely human and on the basis of his personal encounter with God in the Bible, Karl Barth insists, in his lectures and writings, that God is God and man is man. God is totally other, totally different from man. Barth opposes every kind of natural theology, that found in Thomism as well as that found in Protestantism. Catholic theologians who have carefully studied Barth's writings believe that he misunderstands Thomistic philosophy and other Catholic notions, that in a few places he is closer to the core of some Catholic doctrines than he realizes. But since we do not have space here to discuss these agreements and divergences in minute detail, we can only give the general outlines. Barth claims that there is no analogy of being between God and man, that God in no way reveals Himself through nature. Barth will move in only one direction: from God to man. He refuses to see any truth value in moving upward from man to God. God spoke and acted; the record of this is in the Bible. Karl Barth believes that the biblical message is, in a sense, like a foreign object thrown at man, an object from outside man's nature, not a message somehow shaped to man's nature and existence. His theology is called "dialectical" because these two irreducible polar points, man and God, give rise to two different sets of propositions. Man's reason is not a bridge of any sort across the infinite gap that lies between man and God. The propositions that man develops cannot be reconciled with the propositions that God pronounces. Hence, the element of paradox that is ever present in Christian theology and the unending dialogue that must exist. Barth's theology is also called a theology of "crisis" because it makes religion a purely personal encounter between God and man in a social and intellectual wilderness. Man is thus always to be considered under the judgment of God.

Karl Barth is obviously diametrically opposed to the teachings of the liberal theologians. He reinstated some of the basic notions of Calvin and Luther, such as the doctrines that man is in his very nature essentially evil and that man is not justified through good deeds but only by faith in Christ. Karl Barth furthermore rejects the thinking of Protestant theologians like Paul Tillich, who find God to be the answer to various profound problems of human existence. The Barthian God is indeed inscrutable, incomprehensible, unable to be conceptualized in any way whatsoever. All attempts to comprehend and conceptualize God will only mislead men. Man must have faith. Man can meet God in the Bible and nowhere else. Without faith there is mere chaos.

In order adequately to comprehend Barth's motivations, assumptions, and lines of reasoning, one should know, in addition to the thought of Luther and Calvin, something of European intellectual history, especially the epistemology of Kant and the religious existentialism of Kierkegaard. It may at first seem that Immanuel Kant (1724-1804) lived so long ago that there would be no need to mention him in a discussion of basic trends in twentieth-century Protestant theology in Germany. But his tremendous influence on German philosophical and theological thought was of such a basic nature, and so radically different from Thomism, that one must at least have passing acquaintance with his epistemology to appreciate the assumptions of those influenced by him. The question to which Kant addressed himself was the possibility and validity of human knowledge. He concluded that things as they are in themselves cannot be known by human reason. He further stated that human thought is not shaped by extramental objects but that, on the contrary, these external objects depend for their meaning and significance upon the organization of the human mind. Since only man's mind, according to Kant, imposes order and meaning upon the extramental world, it seemed obvious to German Protestant theologians, who studied his writings, that man's reason could not find God through a study of Nature and historical experiences. Nevertheless man does find God. Man finds God because he knows and seeks God through an inner necessity. Hence, Kant became a philosophical support for the Protestant theological tendency to divorce reason from faith.

Søren Kierkegaard (1813-1855) rebelled against the impersonal evolving absolute of Hegel, and against the bureaucracy of the Lutheran Church in Denmark, to champion the suprarational and paradoxical nature of faith. He stressed the infinite qualitative difference between God and man. Religion for him was a personal encounter with God, an existential dialogue. It is easy to see the relationship between the religious existentialism of the anguished Kierkegaard and the crisis element in the theology of Barth. The notion of a religious dialectic was also developed by Kierkegaard.

Even for those who know well his intellectual antecedents, Barth's complex theology, which he has elaborated in over twelve thousand pages of dense writing, cannot in justice be neatly summarized. And its effects too are varied, depending upon the aspect of his thought which is emphasized. His influence in Germany, where he taught from 1921 to 1933 and where his writings are read by both Protestant and Catholic theologians, is greater than it is in Switzerland. His theological influence is not restricted to the Reformed Church, which is small in Germany, but reaches Lutherans with great force. Some Lutherans object to this Calvinistic impact, but in general it can be said that Karl Barth has helped to recall German Protestants to a serious consideration of God as God, to a study of dogma, to a study of the Bible in the light of faith, to interiority. He has brought the theology of the Reformation into the twentieth century. As Pastor Goethe says in this book: "Karl Barth has turned Evangelical theology right back to the absolute theonomy of Luther. . . ."

Of course, there were also other movements against the liberal drift. In the nineteenth century a few Protestants tried to restore to the consciousness of their coreligionists a sense of the importance of the Church as the nucleus of their spiritual lives, emphasizing the liturgy and the sacraments. Not much came of this attempt at that time, but later, a year after the great Reformation Jubilee of 1917, six pastors founded the "High Church Union" which began to publish the small periodical *Die Hochkirche*. Pastor Martin Giebner, who joined this Union in 1921, summarizes in this book many of their proposals and accomplishments. In 1929, this Union elected Friedrich Heiler, a professor at the University of Marburg, as its president. Heiler, who in 1919 had left the Catholic Church and become a Protestant, thought of himself as somehow serving the Church of the future, a Church which could be called "The Church of the Spirit," "The Church of Love," or "The Church of Evangelical Catholicity." While Heiler did publish many articles and books, his chief work was done quietly without publicity. He wanted to be a Catholic without being a Roman Catholic. In 1930, when the anniversary of the Augsburg Confession of 1530 was being celebrated, Heiler bewailed the disintegration of Lutheran theology that had occurred since the time of that declaration by Luther and Melanchthon. Heiler, whose students pay tribute to him for his profound love, did not seek to convert people from one Church to another but tried to lead them to the fullness of the Christian religious tradition. He was seriously concerned about the sacrament of holy orders and about Apostolic Succession.

The German High Church movement did not reject the Reformation, but it did strive to regain some of the religious content which the Protestants had lost during the centuries. It did not aim at reunion with the Catholic Church; it was meant as a sincere attempt to regain more of the pre-Reformation beliefs and practices. If the Catholic Church had liturgical and other religious treasures which belonged to the full Christian tradition, then, said Heiler, one should not hesitate to adopt again these practices. The fact that the

Catholic Church preserved these spiritual riches should make others grateful, not leary. Thus the aim was to Catholicize, in the noninstitutional sense of the word, the Protestant religion. It is interesting to read what Pastor Giebner has to say about the doctrinal and liturgical adoptions they did make.

Needless to say, the High Church Union (which in 1947 changed its name to "Evangelical Ecumenical Circle") had considerable influence in creating a climate more favorable to an examination of the Catholic Church. Many participants in the movement found new riches while remaining Protestants; a few have found the Catholic Church. Pastor Klünder, later in this book, writes: "My first experience of the appeal of the ancient Catholic liturgy took place on October 31, 1922, when a 'German Mass' was celebrated in the Protestant Church of St. Nicholas in Berlin . . . during an annual conference of the High Church Movement. . . ." And Pastor Giebner writes: ". . . I thank, after God, the High Church Union for my 'theological existence today'. . . ." Thus, while one regrets Heiler's own departure from the true Church, one also sees that God can write straight with crooked lines.

An important Evangelical youth movement, which is mentioned by Pastor Goethe, was developed by Wilhelm Stählin, later bishop of Oldenburg, who in recent years has written outstanding articles and books on symbolism and on the catholicity of the Church. The movement was called the Michael Brotherhood. In addition to other activities common to youth movements, they made a thorough study of their Protestant heritage. Somewhat to their surprise, they came to understand that many of the beliefs and practices of

Luther had been dropped over the centuries by the Lutheran Church. They therefore, coming closer to Luther, reintroduced parts of the liturgy, chant and even confession into their worship. They also challenged the bourgeois values prevalent in their society. The Michael Brotherhood as a formative factor was of tremendous importance for many Protestant leaders of the Nazi and postwar years.

It would be misleading to present the situation only in terms of trends favorable to a return to the substantial religious content of the sixteenth century. The age of liberal theology is indeed dead in Germany, but there are other currents besides Barthianism and the High Church movement and liturgical revivals. The name of Rudolf Bultmann is well known and his teachings illustrate another facet of the German Protestant situation.

Bultmann, now a retired professor in Marburg, was famous in the 1920s and 1930s for his method of analyzing the Gospels in terms of the literary forms used. But his greatest fame began in 1941 with the publication of an article on the necessity for "demythologizing" the Gospels. This was not meant in the sense of the earlier liberal theologians. Bultmann did not concern himself with the historical personality of Jesus nor did he aim to portray Jesus as an ideal natural man. He emphasized that Jesus did not teach merely about the development of man toward a social ideal but that Jesus spoke rather about the coming kingdom of God, which was not man's achievement but God's gift. This message that Jesus delivered nineteen centuries ago is the message which is still important today. But it bothered Bultmann that the Gospels were dressed in the cultural

garb of their time, which included miracles and other notions which modern men are apt to reject as superstitious.
These cultural forms and notions are not of our culture and,
according to Bultmann, they have no relevance to Christ's
message. One must therefore separate the message of the
Gospels from the mythology in which it is encrusted. This
task is the process of "demythologizing." Influenced by
Heidegger and other existentialist thinkers, Bultmann
stresses the importance of making personal decisions that lift
one above the brutes and that genuinely fulfill man, but he
dismisses the historical aspects of Jesus. Bultmann has said
that the history of Jesus is not really a part of the history of
Christianity since He was a Jewish prophet and Christianity
only began with the Resurrection. Critics point out that
Bultmann, in effect, rejects the affirmation that "the Word
became Flesh" and approaches the heresy of Docetism, which
makes Christ merely an idea.

Bultmann thinks that the faith of the Christian should
not be tied down to the imagery of the New Testament.
More profoundly spiritual than the liberal theologians, Bultmann is nevertheless extremely disturbing to the Christian
mind. He claims that the phraseology of the Gospels is mostly
symbolic but he insists at the same time that the God-Act
which is there recorded—God's revelation in Christ—is real.
This dichotomy probably sounds ridiculous to one who is
not acquainted with Kantian epistemology and the Protestant distinction between the Jesus of history and the Christ
of faith. To most German Protestant theologians it is not
ridiculous but it is untenable. The dividing line that Bult-

mann draws between myth and truth seems rather arbitrary. This brings up the question again: Who in the Protestant Church decides what is the message of the Bible? Several Lutheran bishops in Germany have spoken against Bultmann's extreme views. But in German Protestantism the individual theology professors at the universities have in the past assumed the right to decide what is true and what is false. Thus, even the extreme teachings of Bultmann can turn some Protestants to a more profound search for the true interpretation of the Gospels and ultimately to the basic question: Who possesses the decisive teaching power?

The Nazi impact upon Protestantism

The theological developments within Protestantism are not the only factors that we must consider. The most important socio-political factor in bringing Catholics and Protestants in Germany into contact with each other on the level of religious truth was their persecution by a common enemy, the Nazi regime. The two Churches faced the situation somewhat differently, but basically they learned that against this enemy they shared many truths as Christians with a common commitment. Until the Nazi persecution came in the 1930s, both Churches, in regarding each other, were psychologically oriented toward the past, recalling constantly their centuries of theological opposition. It was a harsh shock to be confronted suddenly with the realization that, at the present time, they were not enemies but allies. Nor were they merely allies out of fear of a common enemy;

they were allies because they shared values and truths. Thus, they perforce became oriented to the present and to the future.

Through a series of historical circumstances as well as through the external consequences of its theology, the Protestant Church in Germany was, since the time of Luther, organized on a regional basis. The ruling prince became the head of the regional Church, as its most distinguished member. The Lutheran Church thus became subordinate to the state. But when the princes lost their power, with the defeat of the Hohenzollern monarchy in 1918, Church government by them was no longer possible. After the war, each regional Church adopted its own constitution. For centuries, each of these Churches had been completely autonomous, but in 1922 the "Federation of German Evangelical Churches" was formed. This federation did not touch the confessional structure of the individual Churches, which remained divided into three groups: Lutheran, Reformed and Union. There was no common creed. It was merely a federation that would represent all the regional Churches in common tasks, especially in their work in foreign countries. After 1933, the efforts of these regional Churches to achieve a greater degree of unity increased, partly because the evil threat of the Nazis loomed large.

Although one may indeed deplore the general cooperation of Christians in Germany with the Nazi aims insofar as they did not touch ecclesiastical interests directly, it is also an accepted fact that the most consistent German resistance to the Nazis came from the Churches, both Protestant and Catholic. In the nature of its structure, the Catholic Church was strong in maintaining the purity of its doctrines and the allegiance of its members. But the Protestant Church was more vulnerable. Its historical connection with the provincial governments, as well as the shifting sands of its theology and the absence of a public teaching authority, left the members of the Protestant Church with no clear vision of what constituted "The Church." If liberal theology had still permeated Protestantism in 1933, as it did in 1900, the case would have been utterly hopeless. When Hitler came to power in 1933, he immediately sought to transform the Protestant Church into an instrument of his government. During the previous year there had already developed a group who wanted to integrate the Christian message with the purposes of the Nazi Party. Hitler was able to send some of these "German Christians" into the regional Churches as a "Fifth Column." One of the more ardent of these was Ludwig Müller who, as early as April, 1933, discussed with Hitler the possibility of uniting the Protestant Churches and coordinating them with the Nazi ideology and aims.

In order better to resist the Nazi encroachments and because it seemed desirable for intrinsic reasons, the Protestant leaders in May, 1933, created the office of a bishop for all of Germany. They selected a good candidate, Friedrich von Bodelschwingen, but he never took office because difficulties ensued with the Nazis. At a synod held in Wittenberg in September, 1933, the leader of the "German Christians," Ludwig Müller, through intrigue, strategy, and Nazi pressure, was elected Reichsbischof, bishop for the whole of Germany. Ecclesiastical affairs were in a sad state then. Resistance came quickly. Pastor Martin Niemöller of Berlin-

Dahlem formed the "Pastors' Emergency League" which, among other things, sent to Müller a protest signed by 6,000 clergymen. The Lutheran bishops demanded Müller's resignation. But Müller was supported by the Nazi Party; and the Party was powerful, whereas the Protestant Church was not even unified.

The "German Christians," with the power of the Nazi Party behind them, took over the government of many regional Churches. Some of the Churches which were not infiltrated by them nevertheless yielded to the demands of the Nazis whenever neutrality was uncomfortable. However, a sizeable number of the Protestant clergy and laity, under the leadership of men like Karl Barth, Martin Niemöller, and Hans Asmussen, resisted political interference. At first their resistance was directed against the Nazis only insofar as they attempted to control church administration and pervert church doctrines. But gradually, they also began to resist the neopaganism of Nazism itself, realizing that not only the freedom of the ecclesiastical society but also the freedom of civil society was a necessary concern of the Christian citizen.

The "Confessing Church" developed out of the Pastors' Emergency League mentioned earlier. In 1934, about 4,000 ministers (one-fourth of the total German Protestant pastorate) belonged to the group that opposed the Nazi version of Christianity. Their opposition to the Reichsbischof was not silent. At their first synod, held in 1934 in Barmen, Westphalia, they proclaimed that they formed the only authentic Protestant Church in Germany. It included Lutheran, Reformed, and Union Churches. In a declaration that became famous, they clarified the issues at stake. In contrast to the "German Christians" who were making the race, nation, and Führer supreme, de-Christianizing and Germanizing religion, making it a mere adjunct of the state, the Confessing Christians in their Declaration of Barmen proclaimed with courage that the truths of Christ and the freedom of the Church were supreme. They rejected as false the doctrine that the Church should shape its message according to the prevailing ideological and political convictions. The Church was only "The Church" to the extent that it confessed and proclaimed the Word of God. The Church, they emphasized, is not a natural community; it is a community created by the Holy Spirit and maintained by the preaching of the Gospel. Thus, a judgment was delivered regarding the German Christians and the Nazi regime, a judgment in the light of the Bible, not on the basis of political expediency. The judgment was a sharp negative. The influence of Karl Barth, who had given the main address at the synod, was evident throughout. The following year he was expelled from Germany and returned to Basel, Switzerland. The Confessing Church in Germany, however, continued to be inspired by him. Many Germans paid tribute to the theology of Karl Barth for its clarification of the issues involved and for its inspirational value to the members of the resistance movement. There is no question about the clarity and courage with which Barth himself opposed the Nazi tyranny before he was expelled. But some doubts have arisen, especially within the last few years, about the adequacy of Barth's theology in clarifying the Christian's position in the face of tyranny.

Martin Niemöller, who along with Barth is considered the great initiator and inspirer of the Protestant resistance, had been a rather nationalistic German during and after the First World War. Not in love with democratic philosophy, he opposed the Weimar Republic. Niemöller supported the Nazis and welcomed the advent of Hitler. He yearned to see a return to the earlier Church-State arrangements. But Hitler disappointed him grievously. Within a few months after the Nazis had come to power, Niemöller actively turned against them, mostly for ecclesiastical reasons. His record of resistance against the various evils of Nazism from the early autumn of 1933 until the end of the war is really admirable. He spoke out with intelligence and courage. He developed the "Brotherhood Councils" which composed an effective underground government of the Protestant Church in opposition to the "German Christians" and the Ministry of Church Affairs. He traveled much to encourage resisters and to inform Christians of the factual state of ecclesiastical affairs in Germany. But by 1937 he was in jail and from there he was sent to a concentration camp until the end of the war.

In 1936, at the synod held in Oeynhausen, the Confessing Church split on the question of the theological value of their creeds. There were those who grouped themselves around the Barthians and stressed the act rather than the content of faith (*fides qua creditur*) and on the other side the Lutherans who stressed the content as well as the act of faith (*fides quae creditur*). Members of both sides in the dispute continued their courageous resistance against Nazi interference with church life. But the Protestant Church did not present a united front such as was displayed by the Catholic bishops. Protestant pastors were thrown to a large extent upon their own spiritual resources. They faced the urgent task of making their threatened congregations understand the doctrinal substance of the Christian religion in order to prevent them from going over to the "German Christians." They could not achieve this by giving antipapal sermons or otherwise castigating the Catholics for alleged doctrinal distortions. Quite obviously, Catholics too were Christians and not enemies. The circumstances invited expressions of solidarity between the two Confessions. They found themselves cooperating in practical affairs connected with surviving under Nazi persecution. When, in 1937, those Protestant Churches not governed by the "German Christians" were put more directly under the control of the government, the image of the Protestant Church as a Church became increasingly dim. However, the bishops and synods continued to protest vigorously against the overwhelming government interference. One must especially mention Bishop Theophil Wurm of Württenberg whose efforts brought him into the foreground of the Protestant resistance after the imprisonment of Niemöller. The Brotherhood Councils continued their difficult work of providing encouragement and communication among the members of the Confessing Church. But leaders were forced into the army and sent to concentration camps. Despite the severities of the persecution, many Protestant ministers and laymen did not waver in their dedication to genuine Christian values.

In 1945, the Protestant leaders assembled at Treysa, near Kassel, to form a new organization of the Protestant Church in Germany. They had a profound sense of unity as a result of the persecution from 1933 to 1945. They quickly agreed upon a preliminary set of procedures and they adopted a new name: "The Evangelical Church in Germany." They had previously used the title of "The German Evangelical Church." The change in the position of the word "German" in the title was meant to emphasize the fact that it was part of a world Church and not a mere national Church. This was a reflection of their bad experiences with the "German Christians" but it also reflected the influence of the growing ecumenical movement in world Protestantism. We should note too that the label "Evangelical" is used to designate Protestants in Germany. They prefer that term because it expresses a positive content rather than merely a protesting function. But in this essay we shall use the terminology common in America.

The administrative road to federation and the choice of a title were easy but the road to spiritual unity could not be found. Some participants at Treysa, especially those who had issued the Declaration of Barmen in 1934, wanted to form a Church united in creed. This group, small in number, wished to wipe out historical divergences. One must not forget that the Lutheran, Reformed, and United Churches all had different doctrinal notions. The Lutherans, who believed in the real presence of Jesus Christ in the Eucharist, did not want to merge theologically with the Reformed (Calvinist) Church members who did not hold this belief. From a doctrinal viewpoint, the Lutherans even wanted a change in the United Church, which had theologies ranging from strict Lutheranism to rigid Calvinism but usually had a theology which was an attenuated Lutheranism. Meetings took place during the next few years to iron out these difficulties. The final result was that the Evangelical Church in Germany is a federation of twenty-eight regional Churches; it is not "a Church" from a theological and legal point of view. It has no common creed of its own. Its members are not individual Christians or congregations but regional Churches and federations of Churches. Nevertheless, the spirit of unity that exists among these groups is greater than it ever was before. The experiences they endured in common during the Nazi era gave them a psychological unity even if not a doctrinal and liturgical unity. The Evangelical Church in Germany represents all the member Churches in their relations with the state but it does not concern itself with doctrinal questions. Theological and liturgical matters are handled by the provincial Churches and by confessional federations.

Although all the regional Churches belong to the Evangelical Church in Germany, some of them in addition belong to other federations. Ten of the thirteen Lutheran Churches formed, in 1948, the United Evangelical Lutheran Church of Germany. This Lutheran group has a common creed; it is indeed a Church. Its main interests therefore lie along the lines of theology and liturgy. Questions connected with the use of a common hymnal, a common catechism, a common order of worship, are settled by it. In recent years, the United Evangelical Lutheran Church has concerned itself with the doctrines of baptism and confession, the Catholic doctrine regarding Mary and other important matters, but it has shied away from making an official pronouncement on the "demythologizing" of the New Testament that has been recommended by Bultmann. It seems unable to assert itself vigorously as a Church with teaching authority for the simple reason that its members do not believe Apostolic Succession has anything to do with bishops. For them "apostolic" refers to correct biblical interpretation.

The experiences of Protestant Church leaders in the Nazi era included compulsory military service, concentration camps, and executions. Those were years when external practices demanded inner resources. The social pressures did not reinforce the old routine acceptance of Christian forms. The youth movements were absorbed into the Hitler Youth. Social activities formerly carried on by the Churches were severely curtailed by the Nazis. Through social circumstances and suffering, many Protestant ministers developed greater interiority than had been the mode. The confusing situation of their fragmented Church, infiltrated as it was by "German Christians," caused them to search for their own Christian foundations. This search for the meaning of "The Church," for a unity of the followers of Christ, for a fuller nourishment of the spirit of man, did not pervade all or even a majority of the members of the Protestant Church. But it touched enough so that one can say it awakened German Protestant leaders to the possibility of a profounder and richer Christian existence.

Catholicism in Germany

The fact that this introductory essay is intended to present the historical context which will enable the reader better to appreciate the autobiographies of these four converts has prompted us to present first the Protestant background. These converts were, after all, formed within the Protestant Church and they stumbled from truth to new truth while still within that Church. They found their way into the Catholic Church gradually. There is no need here to outline the theology of the Church in which they found fulfillment. For Catholic theology does not change its substance with each historical era. Nevertheless, the social aspects of the Catholic Church and the emphasis given to individual doctrines within the total theology do change. They may even vary between different countries. In a few pages, one cannot trace all the interesting features of Catholicism in Germany. It will be useful for us, however, to describe those aspects which Protestants are apt to witness and contact, since the image that others have of Catholicism depends somewhat upon the way in which it manifests itself within a given society.

In the late nineteenth century, German culture was characterized by a liberal and humanistic Protestantism. The national life was being influenced in the political area by the recently organized Catholics in their powerful Center Party. But the cultural—as distinct from political—influence of Catholics remained insignificant. The Catholics generally belonged to the—relatively speaking—lower economic and social classes. The proportion of Catholics represented on university faculties was smaller than their number in the population would have warranted. It is true that the *Görres-Gesellschaft* was formed in 1876 in order to foster scholarship among Catholics, but the fruits of scholarly endeavors do not appear after a mere year or two. The high positions in society and in civil service were filled by Protestants. Catholic literature was merely didactic and moralizing. German Catholics lived in a cultural ghetto at the end of the nineteenth century. This had many explanations, but the important fact to note here is that in the twentieth century things changed.

At the turn of the century, German Catholic theologians expressed themselves courageously in timely essays and books, literary men made critical appraisals of Catholic literature, in many ways Catholics began to emerge from the cultural ghetto into which they had retreated. Herman Schell, theology professor at Würzburg, in his brochure "Catholicism as a Principle of Progress" urged Catholics to develop a spirit of self-criticism and to cultivate the intellectual life among themselves to such an extent that they would, in advance, undermine the attacks of critical enemies. In this essay he quoted Cardinal Manning who deplored the intellectual and cultural deficiencies of the clergy as one of the barriers to the progress of Catholicism in England. In a later publication, "Ancient Faith and New Times," Schell quoted with approval Archbishop Ireland of St. Paul, Minnesota, in regard to the need for a genuine effort to bring the Church and modern times into a new inner unity. These extremely controversial writings stirred German Catholics.

In 1898, Karl Muth wrote: "Is Catholic Literature Up to the Century's Level?" and answered the question with a resounding "No!" The following year he wrote another essay, "The Literary Task of German Catholics." Both essays started a storm of discussion among German Catholics. With collaborators, Karl Muth founded the periodical *Hochland,* which at first had a difficult existence but gained a reputation of unique excellence. These men, by revealing to Catholics a critical but at the same time positive evaluation of the national German culture, shattered the walls of the narrow spiritual world in which Catholics had become content to live. However, the notion that Catholics should take part only in Catholic organizations, should read only Catholic books with a moral message, should mingle only with Catholics, could not be changed overnight.

The political and social achievements of Catholics between 1870 and the First World War were more striking than their cultural and literary accomplishments. The Catholic Center Party, which later became famous and powerful, was naturally weak when it was first officially constituted in 1871. But the *Kulturkampf* waged by Bismarck during the 70s and 80s served to unite German Catholics politically in the Center Party. Later there were efforts to broaden the base so that it would not be strictly a confessional party. As early as 1906, Julius Bachem, in his article "We Must Get Out of the Tower," urged greater political cooperation with Protestants. Most German Catholics at that time, however, objected to the replacement of a Catholic organization by an interconfessional one. They wanted Catholics to have membership in strictly Catholic organizations. In that integralist spirit, German Catholics organized Catholic trade unions and Catholic industrialists' organizations. When speaking about the political and social situation of German Catholics, the "Popular Union (*Volksverein*) for Catholic Germany" with its headquarters in München-

Gladbach cannot be ignored. Established in 1890, it developed into a large organization which in 1930 had over 4,000 branches and half a million members. Its purpose was to study and disseminate Catholic social doctrines. This was done through numerous lectures, discussions and publications. The *Volksverein* attempted to supplement the purely scientific education, spreading a sense of the richness and fertility of Catholic thought. When the empire of the Kaiser came to an end in 1918 and the Weimar Republic was established, the Catholics gained greater political mobility than they had before. Their political influence increased and the alliances of the Center Party became of great importance. The Catholic Center Party furnished the chancellor in eight of the fourteen cabinets between 1918 and 1933, although it held less than ten percent of the seats in the Reichstag. In 1933, the Center Party somewhat ingloriously voted for the Enabling Act which transferred the power of the Reichstag to the Hitler government and soon thereafter proceeded to dissolve itself. But the experiences which its members had during the years of the Weimar Republic, as well as their persecution under the Nazis, prepared them for the development of the interconfessional political party, the Christian Democratic Union, that was formed after the Second World War.

Another important development in German Catholicism during the time of the Weimar Republic was the liturgical renewal. Although one must pay tribute to Austrian contributions, the centers which deserve most credit for this renewal in Germany are undoubtedly the Benedictine abbeys of Maria Laach and Beuron. The monks at Maria Laach, especially, became famous internationally for their scholarship in liturgical matters. They lived the liturgy to perfection themselves and they reached many by their example, their writings, and their lectures. Under the direction of Abbot Ildefons Herwegen, Maria Laach inaugurated numerous liturgical weeks and institutes. The monks reached a great variety of social groups. But their liturgical institutes and their scholarly publications were directed chiefly at priests and intellectuals. It was rightly assumed that the work would spread if these leaders were impregnated with the ideas of the liturgical renewal.

It was the Catholic Youth Movement, *Quickborn,* which centered around the medieval Castle of Rothenfels, that brought the riches of the liturgy directly to the young university people. The members of the *Quickborn* movement were fortunate in having priests of the calibre of Romano Guardini to direct them. In 1918, he had written the *Spirit of the Liturgy* as the first volume in the series "Ecclesia Orans," published by the Abbey of Maria Laach. These young people were not ecclesiastically-minded nor formed in the liturgy when they rebelled against the bourgeois world. Their reaction was rather that of natural and wholesome youth, almost in the spirit of Rousseau, rebelling against a world of false values. This rebellion could easily have been dissipated. But wise priests like Guardini, who had themselves been formed in the fullness of the Catholic tradition at its best, were able to lead these young Catholics into the living richness of the Church. They sought ways to fulfill man as man amid the vast anonymous forces of the modern world. They sought to understand the profoundest aspects of man's nature and his purpose in the universe. In discussions on the Trinity and the life of the faith, these young Catholics found a new depth. Through their participation in the liturgy, they found a new life. In study groups they learned the connection between religion and problems of the social order. The riches of the Church came into contact with their everyday existence. Needless to say, *Quickborn* and all the other Catholic youth organizations were hampered in their activities, and eventually suppressed, when the Nazis came to power. But they had influenced many young people who in later years, especially after 1945, were able not only to revive the youth movement but also to exert some influence on the social life in Germany.

The period between the end of the First World war and the advent of the Hitler regime saw German Catholics make advances in literature and philosophy. Professor Schlier, toward the end of this book, writes: "Of course, I met the Catholic spirit in Catholic literature . . . the Catholic periodical *Hochland* early attracted my interest and clarified many problems." The mention of even a few names will make the reader realize that Catholics had indeed emerged from isolation. Max Scheler (1875-1928), that very paradoxical personality, communicated to university students a love for absolute values and a humility in front of objective reality. He exposed the shallowness of idealistic philosophy and probed, in a phenomenological manner, the mysteries of the eternal in man. His influence was Catholic, even though he himself ended outside the Church. In 1920, Peter Wust (1884-1948) published *The Resurrection of Metaphysics* in which he synthesized some of the more fruitful developments in modern philosophy with the Perennial Philosophy. Theodor Haecker (1879-1945), once a disciple of Kierkegaard, was led to the scholastic tradition by his study of Cardinal Newman. He was convinced that many others would find their way to the Church through scholastic philosophy. Martin Grabmann (1875-1948), through his research, writings and lectures did much to make neo-scholasticism a vital philosophy again. Edith Stein, by a quite different route, had come to the Catholic Church in 1922. Priest-professors like Karl Adam and Romano Guardini, who influenced many people through their writings, lectures, and sermons, made Catholic theology throb with contemporary relevance. The writings of Gertrud von Le Fort, who became a convert in the mid-1920s, were notable contributions to Catholic literature. Her famous *Hymns to the Church* convey the richness of an existence organically linked to the rhythmic sequence of the liturgical year. A large number of names could be listed but the fact is clear enough: Catholic intellectuals in Germany during those years gained inner substance and some degree of academic and literary prestige.

These years of peaceful religious and intellectual growth soon came to an end. Between 1930 and 1933, the authorities of the Catholic Church in Germany took a firm stand against the rising National Socialist Party. The bishops condemned their evil doctrines and forbade Catholics from becoming members of the Party. One must admit that National Socialism at that time was merely a party and it did not take heroic courage to repudiate it. Nevertheless, it did take intellectual and spiritual clarity and this opposition does show that the Catholic hierarchy was not seduced by Nazi notions of race and nation. Political conditions changed when Hitler obtained control of the government on January 30, 1933. It required both vision and courage to oppose the Nazis after that. The hierarchy urged Catholics in the March 5th election to cast their ballots for the Center Party, but less than half of the Catholic voters followed the pleas of their bishops. Election maps, however, show that Protestant support for Hitler in that election was considerably greater than the Catholic support. The Nazis and their collaborators were firmly in power after the March 5th election. Hitler declared on March 23rd, in the Potsdam military church, that he would recognize and protect the Christian Churches. The hierarchy then began to take a more lenient attitude toward membership in the Nazi Party. On March 28th they withdrew their ordinances prohibiting party membership for Catholics. This does not mean that they began to flirt with Nazi doctrines. They continued to condemn the evil ideology. There was no lack of spiritual clarity on the part of the bishops; there was however a lack of clarity how best to deal politically with this organized menace. It is difficult to ascertain precisely why the bishops withdrew the ordinances prohibiting membership in the Nazi Party, but respect for a legally-constituted government and the hope that the Party would undergo inner reforms now that it was saddled with governmental responsibility were two plausible reasons. The notion that Hitler would form a bulwark against Bolshevism was another reason.

The Nazi Party did not change for the better. It began to interfere with the Catholic press, with the *Volksverein,* and with other Catholic social organizations. Despite this, the notorious von Papen, a Catholic, did his best to reassure Catholic leaders that Nazism contained powerful forces that could be used for a religious restoration. Very few Catholics thought the Nazi movement could be baptized but many thought some agreeable arrangement for peaceful co-existence could be found. The fact that the Holy See signed a favorable Concordat with the German Government on July 20, 1933, gave further encouragement to the hope that the spiritual rights of Catholics would not be violated by the Hitler regime. But the Concordat was violated almost as soon as it was signed. The *Volksverein* of Müchen-Gladbach was suppressed. One cannot avoid wondering why the hierarchy did not object more vigorously to the dissolution of this remarkable organization. The Catholic Peace Union, which had been fervently active in preceding years, was destroyed. The Gestapo interfered seriously with Church services; children and their parents were threatened if they continued to attend confessional schools; youth groups were attacked physically as well as verbally and administratively; the press was curtailed. Many went to prison. The bishops urged Catholics not to obey laws that were unjust; at the same time they urged them to obey the other laws faithfully. The bishops did not want to make a complete break with the legal government of their country. But by 1937, the break between the Catholic Church and the Nazi regime was obvious to all. The encyclical *Mit brennender Sorge,* smuggled into the country and distributed to Catholic pastors without being discovered by the Nazis, was read from all the pulpits in Germany on March 21, 1937. But two days later, a letter from the government was sent to all the bishops forbidding them to print or disseminate that encyclical in any manner or form. The papal document had summarized the many violations of the Concordat and reiterated the unacceptable doctrines of the Nazis. German Catholics were urged by Rome to shun the Nazi doctrines and to resist unjust legislation. They were warned too, by their own bishops, among whom Cardinal von Faulhaber, Bishop von Preysing, and Bishop von Galen were the most outspoken. In fact, Bishop von Galen, "The Lion of Münster," became the symbol of resistance for many Protestants as well as for Catholics.

The members of the German hierarchy repeatedly issued and circulated pastoral letters, pleaded with the government to observe the Concordat, protested against Nazi paganism, against the suppression of various groups. The bishops urged disobedience to unjust laws but they did not encourage open rebellion. Even so, thousands of Catholics were sent to prisons and concentration camps for this passive resistance. It is difficult now for us to imagine the many executions and the endless horrors which intrepid souls underwent simply to confess their faith in God as king and redeemer. But it is also difficult, even when one knows the relevant facts, to understand why so few of the good Christians, of either Confession, were willing to take more active and organized steps at an early date against the Nazi tyranny.

When the war came to an end in 1945, the Catholic bishops of Germany assembled at Fulda, as they do each year, to study their present situation and problems. They recalled that they had consistently resisted the encroachments of the state upon the life of the Church. They paid tribute to those who courageously resisted unjust laws and measures. They mourned the many who had fallen. They also regretfully acknowledged that some Catholics had lent support to outright criminal activities. But the bishops did not have to discuss their status and organization as a Church nor did they have to argue about the substance of their faith. The Church had not for one moment floundered as a Church, neither in ecclesiastical structure nor in theological interpretations, even if some individual members may have been weak in personal heroism.

The historical evidence shows that the Catholic Church, as a Church, stood up firmly under the impact of the National Socialist ideology and the Hitler regime. There was little danger that Catholics in Germany would confuse the Church with the state, whereas the distinction between the two was not so clear for German Protestants, accustomed for centuries to a unique alliance with the provincial governments and hence apt to confuse patriotism with piety. Furthermore, the Catholics had learned valuable lessons from the *Kulturkampf* which Bismarck had waged against them. There was certainly no danger that Catholic theology would disintegrate in the face of a nationalist and racist ideology. As early as 1934 several Protestants (we need only mention the well-known case of Karl Thieme) began to see in the Catholic Church the only bulwark of the Christian faith. The Protestant tradition lent itself easily to nationalism and to complete obedience to the civil ruler; the Catholic tradition tended toward international universalism and kept a clear distinction between the authority of the Church and the authority of the state. All this does not necessarily imply that individual Catholics were more heroic than individual

Protestants when confronted by difficult choices. But it does mean that the image formed of the Catholic Church in the minds of Germans was a clearer, brighter one, with the virtues of unity, stability, and consistency.

The passive resistance of both Churches, carried on quietly by many thousands of individual Christians as well as more publicly by their leaders, was indeed admirable. Individuals learned to help each other as Christians, regardless of the Church to which they belonged. The active resistance groups, such as the famous Kreisau Circle, consisted of members of both Churches. In these small dedicated groups, Protestants and Catholics gained increased respect for each other as Christians. This is one source of the great interest in interfaith discussions in Germany today. Men who had planned together in resistance groups and men who had suffered together as Christians in concentration camps were painfully aware that their disunity was an insult to Christ and a weakness in the face of the enemy.

Many features of the Nazi era fostered among Protestants and Catholics a vivid awareness of the fact that they shared Christian beliefs and values in a world increasingly non-Christian. They no longer looked upon each other as opponents. Catholics realized that Protestants were not merely anti-Catholic but that they too loved Christ and were willing to suffer for Him. The satanic Nazi movement forced thoughtful people to reflect on the nature of their own persuasions. Once the Nazis had consolidated their victories over the Christian social organizations, which fell one by one, neither of the Christian Churches could carry on its varied external activity. They were thus restricted to the more interior spaces of Christian existence. As cultural and social expressions disappeared, the essentials of the Christian religion were more clearly seen by the Christian individual. Compulsory restrictions indirectly helped to illuminate what was central and what was peripheral. The Catholics enjoyed more religious substance. The liturgical movement, which started in the monasteries and next spread to the university student groups, now enriched Catholic parish life. The widespread use of the Schott missal and the adoption of the "German High Mass" are two good illustrations of this. The "German High Mass" receives its name from the fact that, while the celebrant reads and sings his part in Latin, the people sing their parts, both proper and ordinary, in the German language, partly in direct translation, partly in paraphrase. Rome recognized this as a legitimate German custom in 1934. When the need for individual resources was overwhelming or the celebration of the Mass was impossible, Catholics turned to the reading of the New Testament to a greater extent than they would have in normal times. They read it too when they were in groups with Protestants since they had the Bible in common. Thus Catholics, who hitherto had been chiefly nourished by the sacrament of the altar and the piety that grew around it, experienced anew the spiritual vitality that could be found in the Word of God which came to them in the Bible. They learned to appreciate Protestant spirituality too. Thus, from the most varied aspects of human existence, developments conspired to bring the members of the two Christian Churches closer together. We must now examine the contemporary men and movements that help or hinder this movement toward union.

Men and movements today

At the end of the Nazi period, Protestants and Catholics
of Germany had broken some of the psychological barriers
of the past but the theological differences remained. Long
before World War II, the Catholic priest, Dr. Max Metzger,
had encouraged a movement to break down the barriers between Christians arising from differences in belief. Others
had started it but Dr. Metzger gave it verve. He called together a dozen Catholics and a dozen non-Catholic Christian
leaders to discuss in fraternal charity their basic religious
beliefs. It was hoped that this creation of an atmosphere of
mutual good will and a sincere dialogue would eventually
remove the scandal of disunity among Christians and bring
all Christians into One Holy Universal Church. Hence, the
name *"Una Sancta"* was given to this association. Father
Metzger carried on his work from various places, including
Berlin, but the chief center was the House of Christ the
King in Meitingen, near Augsburg. By 1939, the interest in
the movement had grown to such an extent that branches of
Una Sancta had been opened, on local initiative, in most of
the larger cities of Germany. The center in Meitingen published literature on the movement and distributed it to the
numerous branches. A Circular Letter regarding the interconfessional dialogue was issued regularly.

Unfortunately, Father Metzger was executed by the Nazis
in early 1944. But the Sisters of the Society of Christ the
King in Meitingen carried on the work from that center,
the Circular Letters gradually expanded into a quarterly
periodical with the title *Una Sancta*, and the small local

groups of the movement (now a movement rather than an organization), carried on their work throughout Germany. The basic aims of the *Una Sancta* movement included the reduction of prejudices that became traditional through the centuries, the study of beliefs which are mutually held by Protestants and Catholics, the recognition of the positive Christian values in some of the beliefs and practices of Protestants, and the establishment of programs which will enable divergences to be examined fruitfully.

The *Una Sancta* movement flourished wonderfully in the early postwar years. It was an attempt to promote understanding, not to recruit converts. It had splendid success in bringing together Christians of different Churches for serious discussions. But at some of the local conferences rash and imprudent statements were made, mostly by well-intentioned but ill-instructed laymen. Profound theological doctrines cannot be discussed with the democratic casualness of municipal politics. The Holy Office with its *Monitum* of June 5, 1948, temporarily suspended most *Una Sancta* activities. In its Instruction *Ecclesia Catholica* of December 20, 1949, the Holy Office pointed out the various deviations from the truth which had occurred at those meetings. Among the errors the most significant for us to consider is the fact that some Catholic participants in the interconfessional discussions assumed that the One Holy Church would gradually be formed sometime in the future. This idea pervaded the unity movement taking place at world-wide conferences. The Holy Office made it clear that the Catholic Church *is* the One Holy Church. Christianity is indeed divided, but the Church of Christ is not divided. An *Una Sancta* movement is possible and desirable but there must be selectivity in membership, since untrained persons are in no position to discuss these matters, and there must be clarity about the goal, since it is not permissible for Catholics to speak of a new future Church. The Instruction encouraged further efforts but stressed that henceforth the movement would have to be guided and the participation of the general public in discussions be limited. Many Protestants, including Bishop Wurm, refused to cooperate thereafter because they felt that the conclusion of the discussion was determined in advance by the Catholics and that therefore it was impossible to have a genuine dialogue. But other Protestants, including the liturgical-minded Bishop Stählin and the resourceful Hans Asmussen, realized that, even within a restricted framework, the careful examination of their mutual agreements and divergences was bound to be an enriching experience. They indeed developed greater respect for the Catholic Church for its unswerving insistence on the true nature of the Church of Christ. The Catholic Church did not sway with the winds of opinion.

Thus, the crisis of 1948-49 was overcome without disintegration and the movement began anew, in accordance with the Instruction, stronger and surer than before 1948, even if not involving quite so many participants.

Each year the *Una Sancta* Conferences are organized. Each Catholic diocese in Germany has a specialist in these affairs who reports regularly to his bishop. Archbishop Jaeger of Paderborn is the head of the *Una Sancta* Commission of the German Bishops Conference. He has also established the Johann Adam Möhler Institute in Paderborn for the study of ecumenical questions. Each year in January, during the Chair of Unity Octave, lectures are held before hundreds and even thousands of listeners in public halls in most of the cities of Germany. This brings the problems and the ideal of unity to the attention of a wider public. Occasionally these lectures are given greater publicity by being broadcast over the radio. The best-known are the two lectures given on January 22, 1957, over the West German Radio station in Cologne by the Catholic, Monsignor Robert Grosche, and the Protestant, Dr. Hans Asmussen, on the topic: "Do We Need a Pope?" These lectures were published and thus received further attention. Every Thursday evening *Una Sancta* members say special prayers. The members are quite conscious that in a religious movement it is religious prayerfulness and not mere public relations that is important. The quarterly, *Una Sancta,* which has grown from less than fifty pages per issue five years ago, to about one hundred and fifty pages per issue now, is edited by the young Benedictine scholar, Father Thomas Sartory, of the Abbey of Niederaltaich. Father Sartory lectures in many parts of Germany, meets numerous leaders of both Confessions for conferences, and writes devoutly and learnedly on the relevant theological questions. A book by him, *The Ecumenical Movement and the Unity of the Church,* will appear in English translation this fall. The monks at the Abbey of Niederaltaich have established a center for interconfessional discussion where guests, who are always welcome, can live in the monastery in quiet private meditation or join the Benedictines at worship, or participate in discussions. It is interesting to note, by way of illustration, the announcement in the latest issue of *Una Sancta* that in August, immediately after the Protestant *Kirkentag* congress in Munich, there will be a five-day meeting at the Abbey to discuss "The Relationship of Scripture and Tradition in Its Significance for an Ecumenical Council."

Thus the *Una Sancta* movement in quiet ways continues to prepare the way for a more harmonious theological relationship between members of the two Christian confessions. The articles, lectures, and discussions clarify many of the individual doctrines so the increased mutual understanding sometimes brings surprising nearness. But there remains the basic division: for Catholics the *Una Sancta Ecclesia* is already with us, whereas for the Protestants it is an ideal whose realization belongs to the future.

Scholarly historians and theologians in Germany have contributed their share to the creation of better understanding between members of the two Churches. Catholic as well as Protestant scholars during the past thirty years have gained a more objective appreciation of the forces at work in the sixteenth century's religious revolt. An excellent example is the brilliant and scholarly book, *The Reformation in Germany,* by a Catholic priest, Josef Lortz, which appeared in 1940. Professor Lortz swept aside all apologetic purposes and tried to assess the situation at the time of the Protestant Revolt as objectively as possible. Naturally he did not assume the biases of the Protestants simply because he dropped the biases of Catholics. But many Protestants were agreeably surprised that a Catholic priest would write so sympathetically and objectively. Lortz was able to take a sympathetic view of Luther insofar as he rebelled against inexcusable ecclesiastical abuses and also insofar as he sought to find a fulfilling spiritual existence. Luther said some things which needed saying at that time and he was not completely wrong in his criticisms. The philosophical underpinnings which some Catholic teachers gave to theology during Luther's time were indeed questionable. And so Lortz did not start his book with a condemnation of Luther nor did he proceed to ridicule him. The doctrines that Luther espoused were carefully assessed by Lortz for the truth they contained. And they did have substantial truth. What was wrong was that they were torn out of their context, they were exaggerated; mere parts of a larger synthesis were erected into a lopsided system. In thus removing these doctrines from their meaningful framework, Luther distorted them. But those who reacted against Luther were also apt to distort Catholic theology to some extent because they, as is common in polemics, emphasized to the extreme those truths which Luther denied and they minimized some truths which Luther correctly upheld but falsely exaggerated. Thus, the theologies of both sides, the Protestant more than the Catholic, were presented in a way partly determined by the fact that they were pitted against each other. The relaxation of tensions which had occurred in the twentieth century should allow a calm re-examination of the issues at stake in the sixteenth century. Thanks to social changes and theological trends, many Protestants during and after the Nazi period were indeed ready to take another look at their own origins. Professor Lortz did not justify the revolt of Luther. Quite the contrary. Rupture was not a solution to abuses. The abuses in the Catholic Church in the early sixteenth century—the external-ity, superficiality, and emotionalism—can hardly be imagined by devout Catholics today. These abuses, once recognized and acknowledged by Catholics, can be dismissed, especially since it is obvious that the abuses against which Luther revolted no longer exist in the Catholic Church. We can then face the spiritual questions in terms of reality, not in terms of prejudices and antagonisms. Lortz's sympathetic study and his evident knowledge of Protestant scholarship on Luther helped to reduce mutual prejudices and did much to further the dialogue between contemporary Christians. In his present position as director of the Institute of European Studies in Mainz, seventy-year-old Professor Lortz, with the help of scholarly young collaborators, is continuing his fruitful revisionist studies in Reformation history.

Another Catholic priest-professor who has by learned writings and lectures contributed much to the interconfessional dialogue is Karl Adam of the University of Tübingen. He is now rather inactive, since he is eighty-three years old, but his many lectures during his years as professor of dogmatic theology as well as his books have given him international renown as a scholar of breadth, profundity, and vitality. One of his books, *The Spirit of Catholicism,* which has become a world classic since its publication in 1924, is mentioned by Pastor Goethe as influential in his own approach to the Catholic Church. In 1947, Karl Adam delivered three stimulating lectures to a large gathering of the *Una Sancta* movement. In Germany they were published under the title *Una Sancta from the Catholic Viewpoint* but in English translation the book was entitled *One and Holy.* In these lectures, Professor Adam first traces the roots of the Reformation and the manner in which Luther left the Catholic Church. He then examines the possibilities of reunion. The first step, he thinks, is to bring Lutherans today back to the doctrines of sixteenth-century Lutheranism. Since Martin Luther left the Church for subjective reasons, it seems to Adam that it is necessary to focus the attention of Lutherans upon the person of Martin Luther, show them that his subjective reasons for leaving the Church are no longer valid, and thus lead them into the Church of Luther's youth. This process requires the development of certain attitudes. Karl Adam emphasizes the necessity of softening the antagonisms that exist between believers without concealing the real differences in doctrine. In this regard, he notes that Protestantism, because it had critically to condemn Catholic doctrines in order to justify its own existence, has developed unjustified antagonism to a greater degree than Catholics. Protestant leaders who are interested in developing mutual understanding must work diligently to root out that bad habit. But Catholics too must not forget to supplement the dogmatic intolerance of their Church with genuine openness of heart and true charity. Karl Adam's book is an excellent introduction for any person who wants to learn more about the content and manner of the *Una Sancta* dialogue.

While the *Una Sancta* movement has dedicated participants from both Churches, its basic inspiration and its general complexion comes from Catholics. Some Lutheran ministers with a Catholic yearning have developed their own movement, addressed chiefly to Protestants. The leading members of this movement became aware of each other during the postwar years through reading each other's articles, in various periodicals, on topics of theological and liturgical reform within Protestantism. Gradually they met each other personally. By 1954, they were writing long Circular Letters which they sent to Protestant ministers in Germany, Austria, and Switzerland. In this way they hoped to make contact with others who were interested in this reform. Twice a year, they organized meetings that lasted several days, at which interested persons could hear lectures and join in the discussion of these controversial topics. The association of leaders in this endeavor took the name "The Gathering" (*Die Sammlung*), derived from the words of Christ: "He who does not gather with me, scatters" (Matthew 12:30). Much smaller than the *Una Sancta* movement, The Gathering nevertheless has a following of over a thousand Protestants and contacts with a few hundred interested Catholics. But the only Protestant group that has shown genuine interest is the Michael Brotherhood. Nevertheless, The Gathering has religious influence. In 1958, they published a book entitled *Catholic Reformation,* which contains the seven Circular Letters and additional chapters written by the men most important in The Gathering, including Hans Asmussen, Max Lackmann, and Richard Baumann. We already mentioned Hans Asmussen in connection with the Confessing Church. It has been reported that the German Order of Merit was recently conferred upon him for his work in the resistance against Nazi interference. He is a Lutheran minister of great ability and deep spirituality, who has in the past held high offices in the Lutheran Church and in the Council of the Evangelical Church in Germany. Pastor Baumann a few years ago began to preach his conviction that the See of Peter has valid claims to the allegiance of all Christians. Since every pastor is presumably free to interpret Scriptures, Baumann saw no reason why he should not expound his own serious interpretation. But for this un-Protestant interpretation he was dismissed from his ecclesiastical office and cut off from his rights and his salary by his regional Church. He wrote an interesting book on the affair a year ago. Pastor Lackmann in recent months has also been dismissed from his parish, although many testified to the fact that he prudently knew how to distinguish between learned theological disputations and the spiritual guidance of his simple flock. These men in The Gathering are willing to suffer for their beliefs. It is therefore especially interesting to read their book, *Catholic Reformation,* which is soon to appear in English translation in the United States.

The writers of that book deplore the notion, all too frequently held, that the Protestant Church began in 1517. In reality, it has the previous fifteen centuries of Christian existence in common with the Catholic Church. In studying their own history, Protestants cannot begin in 1517. If it is desirable to have a full Christian existence, then it is necessary to have a Catholic Reformation within the Protestant Church. This refers to the need for recovering the common Christian heritage; it is not immediately a question of reunion with the Roman Catholics. A study of the Augsburg Confession of 1530 is a good way for Protestants to learn about the great amount of Catholic content that their own Church had at that time. Questions about the powers of the bishop's office, about the Mass and the sacraments will then naturally arise. In fact, some of the attempts that have been made to restore

greater sacramental life in the Lutheran worship have met
with resistance, not among the people, but among the
leaders. "Is this not strange?" ask the members of The
Gathering. They go on to affirm their belief that the Catholic question is the most important question of our generation. But this question will not be solved by "unconditional
surrender" to the claims of the Catholic Church. The
Gathering cooperates with the *Una Sancta* movement but it
has different notions about the shape of the eventual reunion. The way is not seen clearly, but perhaps, they think,
there may eventually be room for the Lutherans as a feder-
ated body within the Church. The book goes on to discuss
the need for Catholizing the Evangelical Church and then
expounds on the Catholic elements that exist in the New
Testament, in tradition, in the episcopal office. If Karl
Adam's book is an excellent introduction to the *Una Sancta*
dialogue, this book, *Catholic Reformation,* by The Gathering, is a splendid introduction to the Catholicizing movement within the Protestant Church.

There are other Protestant movements in Germany that
try to foster a better understanding of Catholicism. A large
number of Ecumenical Institutes to study controversial topics
of ecclesiology and theology have been established in connection with theological faculties. In a library and reading
room they make available the significant writings of every
important Christian theologian. The Lutheran Church in
Germany as early as 1952 recommended to pastors that they
promote the private confession of sins. In the summer of
1956, at the Protestant *Kirchentag* in Frankfort, one of the
speakers exhorted the audience to make use of confession.

After this speech, by popular demand, eight Protestant ministers were busy hearing the private confessions of penitents. In speaking about repentance, one thinks also of the penitential Protestant Sisterhood that was established in 1947 in a suburb of Darmstadt. These semicontemplative nuns want to atone for the evils of the Nazi period, especially for the sins committed against the Jews. The name of this order, The Ecumenical Sisterhood of Mary, indicates the renewed devotion that some Lutherans have to the Mother of Jesus Christ. Bishop Stählin and Hans Asmussen, among others, have written appreciatively about the role of the Virgin Mary. It is certainly not unconnected with German developments that the Lutheran World Federation decided, at their Minneapolis meeting in 1957, to establish a special world-wide center to study, among other religious questions, Roman Catholicism. Bishop Hanns Lilje, of Hanover, who was at that time the President of the Lutheran World Federation, pointed out that the relationship of their Church to the Catholic Church has to be re-examined anew by every generation. Steps have been taken to set up the proposed new world-wide center and it is scheduled to be headed by a Danish Lutheran, K. E. Skydsgaard, whose specialty is in the area of the Catholic-Protestant dialogue.

On the other hand, there are many Protestants in Germany who seek unity but who are not enamored of so-called "Catholicizing tendencies." They find their expression in the general Protestant ecumenical movement which started in 1910 with a conference in Edinburgh and achieved complete structural organization with the creation of the World Council of Churches at the assembly held in Amsterdam in

1948. The initial impulse had come from the Protestant missionaries who found themselves hampered in their work by the fact that there were about 250 versions of Christianity. It occurred to them that unity in doctrine would make missionary efforts more effective. But at a later conference in Sweden the participants thought they could achieve unity more easily if they would ignore divergences in doctrines of faith and questions of ecclesiastical and liturgical order and would instead devote themselves to practical problems of life and work. Thus, there developed two parallel movements, each seeking unity but seeking it on different grounds: the Faith and Order movement sought unity in doctrine whereas the Life and Work movement tried to achieve unity in practical matters. But questions regarding faith and order could not be dismissed even when practical tasks were being discussed. In 1948, the leaders of these movements joined other Protestant leaders to form the World Council of Churches. This World Council has over 160 member Churches, representing more than 160,000,000 believers. Everyone will grant that it is quite an achievement to unite 160 churches. But in what way are they united? The World Council has no doctrine of its own, except that implied by the very general statement that it is a fellowship of Churches which accept Jesus Christ as God and Saviour. It is not a super-Church. It can neither impose doctrines nor make laws for member Churches. The World Council does provide the opportunity for developing united action in matters of common interest. It calls conferences on world and regional levels to discuss subjects that are of importance and relevance for a council of Churches. While this present state of the World Council does not indicate large areas of doctrinal unity, many of its members hope that greater unity will come. A few silently nourish the hope that it may some-day grow into a unified Christian Church with one doctrine. This path to unity among Christians, which is not the Catholic Church's way, has great appeal to Protestants. The unified Church of the future which they envision would not be a gathering around an already existing Church, it would not be a return to an earlier ecclesiastical order. It would be a new institution. This approach seems democratic to Protestants who, for the most part, think of a Church as primarily a fellowship of believers. The Catholic Church should then, they think, deal with the World Council of Churches and come to an agreement with that organization on how they could eventually merge into one. A few Protestants have been irked by Pope John's call for a world-wide council to discuss Christian unity, because to them it seems that His Holiness ignores the great work that has been done by the Protestant ecumenical conferences. Those who react in that manner, however, betray their superficial understanding of the situation, since they evidently fail to comprehend the deeper causes of the differences between the Catholic and the Protestant approaches to unity. It is, of course, easy to see that those Protestants who are fond of the World Council of Churches' approach to unity would not be attracted to the path offered by the *Una Sancta* movement nor especially interested in the efforts of The Gathering, although a few persons (e.g., Hans Asmussen) belong to all three movements. Many German Protestants look in the direction of the World Council of Churches to satisfy their felt need for greater Christian unity. Repeated disappointments in their Faith and Order discussions will not necessarily turn the participants to the path offered by the Catholic Church.

It would be a mistake to assume that the favorable interest in Catholicism that exists among German Protestants is a widespread mass movement that has become overwhelmingly powerful. Although about ninety-five percent of the West German population are affiliated with one or another of the Christian Churches, a large proportion are merely nominal church members. They are willing to remain subject to the church tax (collected by the state government for the Churches), but they do not associate themselves more closely with their Church. Only about twenty percent of the Germans affiliated with the Protestant Church are regular churchgoers. The other eighty percent are obviously not deeply concerned about the religious enrichment of their Church or about Christian unity. Neither are the majority of the practicing twenty percent ardently interested in the ideal of unity. In fact, there are some outstanding Protestants who indulge in caustic criticism of the Catholic Church.

Martin Niemöller, who became famous for his Christian zeal during the Nazi period, seriously considered becoming a Catholic when he shared a concentration-camp cell with Catholic priests. But in the past ten years he has frequently displayed extreme antagonism toward the Catholic Church. He considers himself a political neutralist who courageously applies the Gospels to the contemporary human situation. However, his critics accuse him of reducing the Gospels to the level of politics. He feels compelled to de-

nounce the Vatican for alleged political manipulations and
expresses considerably greater friendship for East Germany
than for the government of West Germany, which he claims
was conceived in the Vatican and born in Washington. Of
course, Niemöller is in no sense a Communist and he is loyal
to the West German government which he professes to de-
spise. Whatever his value may be in cultivating better relations with fellow Protestants in the Soviet Zone, there is no
doubt that he cannot be counted among those who now help
the cause of better understanding and friendship between
Protestants and Catholics in Germany.

One of the men who has had great influence on Niemöller is Karl Barth, who was so unequivocal in his early
opposition to Nazism but finds it difficult to utter a strong
word against Communism. About a year ago, Barth wrote a
provocative forty-page letter which advocated neutralism
toward the satellite Communist regimes. The letter was
written in response to eight questions sent him by a Protestant pastor from East Germany. A sympathetic reader can
make no serious objection to Barth's discouragement of any
kind of resistance against the Communist government nor
to his recommendation that adversity and suffering be seen
as the instruments of God. But in his letter Barth goes on to
urge the Christians in the Soviet Zone to accept the Communist regime as the will of God, to be thankful for the
freedom they enjoy, and to realize that the political and
social order has no real importance for Christian believers.
An institutionalized Church has little value in his eyes.
Barth shows an unusual affinity for Communism when he
urges the East Germans to see the creative possibilities in

the experiment being tried in their land but can make only disparaging remarks about West Germany. In answer to the question whether it would be in accord with the Gospels to pray for deliverance from the Communist regime, Barth is not decisive, remarking that the prayers might be fulfilled in some awful way, such as waking up one morning and finding oneself obligated to "The American Way of Life." If one ignores the political overtones and looks for the theological principle, it seems that Barth says that the pure Christian should not care about political alternatives because they are all bad. The socio-economic and political level of existence is indifferent to the inner life of the Christian. This kind of abstract impartiality may be fitting for the incomprehensible Barthian God, but men in society find it of little help. Barth's Olympian theological posture results in sheer irrelevance for moral man. This letter by Barth has raised storms of protest in Germany. Those who thought that Barth's theology dictated his resistance to Nazi tyranny now wonder why it does not also inevitably dictate resistance to Communist tyranny. It occurs to some observers that his personal nontheological inclinations rather than his theology served to guide him, both then and now. Barth is somewhat less than a beacon of light in the present struggle for freedom in this human world.

However, most Germans are not loftily indifferent to the Communist tyranny. In a sense, the Communists have taken over the role played earlier by the Nazis in bringing Protestants and Catholics together. This is especially true in East Germany, dominated by a puppet Communist government. The story of difficulties there would take another chapter.

The problem is especially great for the Protestants since the large majority of the eighteen million inhabitants of East Germany belong to that Church, while only a little more than one-tenth of them belong to the Catholic Church. The substitution of various Communist ceremonies for the Christian sacraments of baptism, confirmation, and marriage, the compulsory attendance at antireligious state schools, the numerous restrictions on travel, and the suppression of Christian literature are bravely counteracted by both Protestants and Catholics. Many current periodicals contain detailed accounts of the Communist attempt to paganize youth and the courageous efforts made by Christian leaders to reduce the damage.

Not only in the Soviet Zone, but in West Germany too, the Communists have greatly influenced religious relations. This has been felt especially through the ten or eleven million refugees from Communism that have streamed into West Germany since the war. These refugees of both Confessions scattered all over the country without regard to religious affiliation. In Germany the population pattern had been, as a result of the principle of *"cuius regio eius religio,"* that Catholics clustered together solidly in one geographical region, Protestants in another. These homogeneous religious groupings in different parts of Germany have been shattered by the arrival of refugees. Hence, the religious map of Germany looks rather different today than it did twenty years ago. Catholic refugees who came to Protestant areas found themselves without church buildings. The same was true for Protestant refugees who moved into previously Catholic areas. The two churches therefore offered each other the use of their church buildings. This hospitality had already developed during the war years, when evacuees from bombed cities found themselves in areas settled by members of the other confession. Well over a thousand churches are used by both Protestants and Catholics. If one counts those in East Germany, there are several thousand. This refers to the use of the church building; it does not imply that they have common worship. But the common use of a building is a remarkable indication of the spirit of cooperation and mutual respect that exists between the two confessions. Since thousands of refugees continue to cross the border each month, the intermingling process has not come to an end.

Americans who survey the German religious scene must keep a few other facts in mind. Slightly less than half of the fifty million people in West Germany belong to the Catholic Church, about half belong to the Protestant Church. One half of the Protestants, in turn, belong to the Lutheran Church, the other half to the United Church. The strictly Calvinistic Reformed Church has less than half a million members. The small sects are numerically insignificant. The Lutherans predominate even more than these general proportions indicate, because many members of the United Church adhere to Lutheran doctrines. Thus, there is less fragmentation of Protestantism than there is in the United States. Furthermore, Lutherans in Germany are much closer to Catholics in theology and liturgy than are American Protestants.

In contrast to the United States, there is no Catholic school network. The universities in Germany are state universities. They have theological faculties, both Protestant

and Catholic. Theological students of both Confessions therefore are apt to have some contact with each other and some
knowledge of the theology taught by the other Church.
Pastor Goethe did not find much contact of this sort when
he was a Protestant theology student at the beginning of the
century, but this was either not typical or else the situation
has changed with succeeding decades. Compared to America,
the situation lends itself to much greater knowledge and
contact. At least the theology professors of both Confessions
in Germany are aware of each other. The social and political organizations now also foster more friendly contact
between members of the two Churches than was the pattern
in the past. The interconfessional Christian Democratic
Party receives about one-third of its votes from Protestants.
Within this party there is a spirit of healthy cooperation
among believers of both Confessions. Americans are accustomed to this in their political parties but in Germany it is a
new development. In the area of social action, Catholics
at the beginning of this century had heated controversies
whether they should have separate organizations for themselves or should join with Protestants. This cooperation is
now taken for granted. The controversy has shifted to the
question whether convinced Christians should cooperate
with socialists. The trade unions were organized on a nonconfessional, nonideological basis after the war. Some devout
Christians found this neutrality agreeable and decided to
band together as a voluntary group to exert their influence
within the framework of the neutral organization. These
Christian Colleagues within their circles of lower level
leaders have been able to present with vigor the Christian

social philosophy. Other Christians claimed that the neutrality was really a front for socialism and withdrew in 1955 to
form a separate Christian Trade Union movement. This
splinter development has not attracted a great following.
The neutral unified trade unions are commonplace in
America, but in Germany they too were new developments.
Thus, the political and social organizations of postwar Germany, as well as the traditional state universities, bring
Protestants and Catholics together for fruitful human cooperation in matters of mutual interest.

This brief summary of developments in Germany may
make some readers unduly optimistic. If they will recall the
high hopes aroused by the Oxford movement in the past
century, they may temper their enthusiasm. Since collective
entities obey not only religious impulses but also sociological laws, we can assume that there will be no wholesale
corporate reunion in the near future. Nobody can predict
the course of development during coming centuries. Perhaps
the non-Catholic Christian Churches of the Western world
will continue to be separated from the Catholic Church.
Participants in long-range movements must satisfy themselves with the achievement of limited intermediate goals,
such as the cultivation of a creative peace between Protestants and Catholics. But the principle of the inevitability of
gradualness which dominates the life of social institutions
applies only in a very limited degree to the life of an individual person. An individual Christian can find in his own
lifetime the one true Church and must indeed choose it
once he has discovered it. The four converts, who tell us in
this book the stories of their search and their discovery,

made their personal decisions without waiting for the desired and unpredictable and, at any rate, ponderous movement of the ecclesiastical institutions to which they belonged. We too cannot delegate all responsibility to institutional structures. For the sake of Christian unity, we must pray to God, open our hearts to our fellow Christians and engage in an intelligent dialogue with them. In the words of Karl Adam: "If there cannot immediately be unity of faith, let there at least be unity of love."

RUDOLF GOETHE

The Open Door

IF A RAY of sunshine falls upon a fragment of glass it begins to shine. If God's light shines upon a man's life, he cannot help but reflect that light so that all may see it.

At the request of many and with no light heart I have decided to give an account of my life in an effort to reveal how doctrine develops out of living.

It may convince one or another that God still performs miracles.

I was born in Geisenheim in Rheingau where I came into the world together with my twin brother on December 23, 1880.

My father was related to a distant branch of the family of the poet Goethe in the province of Saxony. When in high school he became an orphan, and was forced to take up the profession of gardener. He made such a success of it that he became an expert on fruit and vine culture, and was well known even outside Germany. As director of the Institute for Horticulture in Geisenheim, his proficiency caused this institution to flourish exceedingly.

My paternal grandfather was a councilor of the board of revenue. We know no more of my grandmother than that she was a clergyman's daughter.

My mother, an energetic Swabian, came from a family of Würtemberg Pietists. Her father was a much-frequented nerve specialist in Cannstatt and a friend of the famous pastor, Christoph Blumhardt of Bad Boll. The latter started a great revivalist movement and healed many sick persons in a wonderful manner by the power of his belief in the validity of the promises of Jesus Christ even for men of today. This

Pietism preserved its simple Bible faith in a period when criticism was making everything appear doubtful. The Swabian hymn writer, Albert Knapp, was my mother's godfather. She was also related to many of the Evangelical clergy of Würtemberg.

With me and my brother, who later became the captain of a frigate, my mother had a great deal of trouble, for from birth we were very delicate children. Surprisingly enough, we have outlived the three older children by many years. Although our mother ruled the nursery, making energetic use of the cane, our house was completely pervaded by a Christian atmosphere. Grace was regularly said at meals, Father read evening prayers from a book of devotions, and, whenever possible, we all went to church on Sundays.

When we were eleven our parents had to send my brother and me away to a boarding school. We never returned there after the holidays without first kneeling to receive our mother's blessing. Once when the bishop of Mainz was visiting Geisenheim for a confirmation, he paid us a visit in order to thank my father for some planting he had supervised for a church establishment. When this high dignitary asked what our religion was, my mother could not help answering in her impetuous way, "We are Protestants and shall always remain true to the faith of our fathers." The bishop, smiling, then blessed us all with the words of the 127th Psalm, "May your children be as olive plants round about your table."

We brothers, who were carefully looked after in the grounds of the school, often had "border struggles" at the gate with the other boys of the little town. Religious differ-

ences played their part in these conflicts, too. I still remember
as though it happened today how when I was in grade school,
I was called out of class and had to appear before the in-
structor of Catholic religion during his class. I trembled as
he sternly lectured me. "You said that we Catholics worship
the Virgin Mary. We do not worship her, but we do honor
her."

I still recall the self-sacrificing Catholic Sisters keeping
watch day and night at our sick beds for weeks on end when
we were children. A Franciscan Father of Mariental, who
had shown a liking for us twins, is another early memory.
How delightful it was when we were permitted to cross the
Rhine in a boat and take part in the famous feast of St. Roch.
The religious ceremonies were a great surprise; but what we
enjoyed most were the hot sausages and the romantic journey
home in the evening.

During my grammar school period in Neuwied, two
things had a great effect upon me. One was a really good two-
year course of instruction for confirmation, and the other the
divine service of the Moravian Brethren, that sincerely devout Pietist community, founded by Zinzendorf. The faithful participated in this service, in a degree that accorded with
their "estate," in special church costumes.

Our confirmation in Rüdesheim, a place with which we
had grown unfamiliar, made no great impression.

As young students at Weilburg an der Lahn, during the
troublesome period of adolescence, I and a friend, who later
became an Evangelical pastor, joined a conversion movement (League for Decided Christianity and White Cross

Purity League), but our participation came to a sudden end
with the mental breakdown and death of a fellow schoolboy
who was also a member.

My decision to study Evangelical theology gave pleasure
to my mother.

A life of happy friendship in a Tübingen students' club,
together with activities such as hiking, riding, swimming,
and fencing, soon loosened up the boy who had been rather
too carefully brought up. Study there and in Halle was in-
strumental in exposing me to theological impressions and
views which I found quite contradictory. How could the
mind of the young student make clear decisions out of the
multiplicity of opinions? How far had Evangelical theology
moved from Luther—via the old-Lutheran orthodoxy, the
conversion theology of Pietism, the Enlightenment, Idealism,
the Romantic movement up to the "humanist" Harnack and
the liberal theology of the school of historical criticism and
the history of religion! At that time Harnack's star was in its
zenith. Contact with the devout biblicists, Schlatter in
Tübingen and Kähler in Halle, had not gone very deep when
Heim, who was my warden in the Silesian hostel, and who
later became the dogmatic theologian of Tübingen, attracted
me to his critical thinking.

In spite of my daily devotions and association with learned
students of theology, this period in the hostel exposed me to
all sorts of temptations in regard to my personal piety. I
began to suspect that prayer might be a sort of auto-sugges-
tion, so I gave up saying my morning and evening prayers
for three months, until at last I found my way back to the
heart of the heavenly Father, feeling quite cold and lonely.

At that time there was no question of any settlement with Catholic theology. I did not make the slightest contact with Catholic theologians at the university. I remember that many of us thought of them as somewhat foreign as a German might think of a Frenchman or an Englishman.

In the Herborn theological college we did not become much more enlightened than before. Of course, the prime purpose of this training was to prepare us for the practical duties of our office. I remember how I toiled at that time with the works of Hollatz, the last dogmatic theologian of "Lutheran orthodoxy." As model sermons I was handed the spirited sermons of the famous English preacher, Robertson. This was the man who "strengthened the courage and the humility of countless men and women, especially in Germany, so that they could experience from their hearts the holy authority of the Redeemer, free from all dogmatic prejudice, in a spiritual surrender to the Son of Man."

I concluded my studies at the seminary and, after three years in the ministry, I did a further year of study at Marburg an der Lahn and found in the dogmatic theologian Professor Herrmann, a Ritschlian, at least a consistent teacher. "Here the whole personality participated in the work of the theologian." For him, making sharp distinctions along the lines of Kant, the only pure knowledge was natural science. He believed that there was no speculative cognition of God; and that there was only a practical way to God through a living encounter with Him as the One Living Being, and therefore that He could only be experienced in historical time. Ethics leads man to come face to face with the law of truth and liberty, whereas religion provides the answer to the fact that man cannot always live in accordance with the moral law, a fact which we learn through our own personal struggles. Although Jesus of Nazareth in Holy Scripture is a historical figure, He who can be truly called "the Living One necessarily cannot either be discovered or set aside by purely historical research." He can only be "experienced" in the encounter with Holy Writ. It is the task of dogmatic theology to express in logical form the answer of the faith of the community to this encounter.

That is it: Jesus Christ in Holy Scripture! . . . But how can one really meet Him there as the One who lives? This question was my constant companion through the first ten years of my pastoral life.

The epoch-making book of Albert Schweitzer, then lecturer in theology at Strasbourg, *Von Reimarus bis Wrede,* meant for me a great liberation from the nimbus of the "Leben Jesu research" and from the so-called "liberal picture of Jesus" represented by Harnack. Schweitzer made a clean sweep of both.

After my conversion, people reproached me with having broken my oath. It is true I was bound by it "to teach pure and undefiled the whole doctrine of the Christian religion, as it is contained in the Holy Scriptures and in the general creeds of the Christian Church as well as in the Reformation confessions of our church, especially in the Confession of Augsburg."

But we felt such an obligation only in regard to the truth which came to us from the "Word of God." Any obligation with regard to the contents of the "confessions" meant little

to us in those days. There was indeed no real inner obligation at a time when people questioned even the binding
character of individual parts of the Apostles' Creed, and regarded the other "confessions" as, at the best, venerable documents of the past.

"The Church herself no longer recognized the 'confessions'
as binding in practice upon all preachers," says Professor
Schlink in his *Theologie der lutherischen Bekenntnisschrif-
ten* (p. 12). This was particularly true during the time of
Harnack, who saw in dogma a fruit of "the Hellenization of
Christianity" and who therefore rejected a Christianity
bound to dogma. In this opinion he resembled Schleier-
macher, the "Church Father of the nineteenth century."

One can still read in a church ordinance, after the experiences of Wars of Reformation, the following sentence,
"The Church must at all times witness to her confessions
testing them obediently in the light of Holy Writ and giving ear to the brethren!"

In principle one was completely free to teach as one liked.
One could even alter the form of the service. "The order of
service is different in every church," an ecclesiastical inspec-
tor told me in 1946. He could have added, too, that every
pastor preaches his own theology.

With these ideas in mind, I took up my office, my heart
full of yearning for real authority, for completeness, for fullness, for the reality of God which supports all things, and
which makes of the preacher a true witness.

Reality? In my first curacy which finally set me in the
stream of life, I came across the reality of death on many occasions. A dreadful epidemic of typhus afflicted my village

(Dotzheim bei Wiesbaden) and caused many deaths. My superior was ill with it and I, the young beginner, was the only pastor in the quarantined area, the only one left to bear the whole spiritual responsibility.

When my father retired and moved to Darmstadt, I transferred from the ecclesiastical province of Nassau to that of Hesse and became "parish assistant" in this town with its wonderfully flourishing youth work.

At twenty-nine, after the study at Marburg mentioned above, I was appointed to my first parish, the little market town of Wörrstadt in the middle of Rhenish Hesse. So-called "free thought" and social democracy were dominant trends in this place. Attendance at church was poor, and people often worked on Sundays. The natives of Rhenish Hesse are indeed a kind and hospitable people, but they are rendered careless and excitable by the wine they produce and enjoy. I therefore adopted abstinence from the beginning. How I exerted myself at that time by means of quite round-about educative methods to make contact with both the young and old! There were exhibitions of pictures and books, labor exchange, theatrical performances in which the church choir participated, meetings with the youth militia, and in 1915, the erection of a local Red Cross hospital.

At the beginning of December, 1916, the war took me for two years to the Western front as a military chaplain to the fighting divisions.

Reality. Yes, here it was again: How often I met death on the road to the trenches, in the attack, in the chief dressing-station or in the hospital! One got to know the meaning of "nation" and "comradeship"! The problem of suffering gave me a terrible amount of trouble. Could God's love, then, permit all these horrors of war, yes, even cooperate in the flight of the grenades? I frequently argued deep into the night with the Evangelical chaplain of our division, a follower of the philosopher Hartmann and also a mystic. A mature Berlin rector eventually was more helpful to me. After a lecture at a conference of field chaplains in Champagne that filled me with despair, he very kindly sent me his delightful and simple book of sermons. But my questions were only resolved much later, when the complete redemption of the fallen world really came to meet me. In general I was on particularly good terms with the Catholic chaplains on the front. For a year and a half I was with an excellent Jesuit father of Westphalia. When we lived for a time in the sacristy of a church which had been turned into a hospital, I was able to hear him rise quietly from his sleeping place below me, wash himself and then say his Mass, while I kept my eyes decently closed in the upper berth. Throughout this whole period, it never occurred to me to exchange one word with my good comrade as to the meaning of this holy rite.

Many times I was permitted to experience the power of the Word of God upon myself and my companions in the greatest hours of trial! Here is just one example: The dentist called me into his tent to see a soldier for whom he had made a new lower jaw in place of the one that had been shattered —highly ingenious! But all I saw before me was a lump of plaster of Paris with a hole in it to permit feeding and breathing. What was I to say to this poor shattered child? I stood there terribly upset. Suddenly these words came from my lips:

> The Lord is my shepherd; I shall not want.
>   In verdant pastures he gives me repose;
> Beside restful waters he leads me;
>   he refreshes my soul.
> He guides me in right paths
>   for his name's sake.
> Even though I walk in the dark valley
>   I fear no evil; for you are at my side
> With your rod and your staff
>   that give me courage.

And from the plaster of Paris tube came the words: "Oh, how beautiful!"

But what remained of that reality I experienced in the field after the sad return home with the defeated army? Well, one thing I recall was a clash with the French occupation forces over some youthful pranks played by home-returning soldiers of my parish who were revenging themselves upon the girls who had been "friendly to the French." This incident resulted in my imprisonment at Mayence, and an appearance before the military court. The splendid hymn of Paul Gerhardt brought great peace to me in my cell on the first evening, faced as I was with the prospect of several years' imprisonment.

> Commit thou all thy griefs
> And ways into his hands,
> To his sure truth and tender care

Who earth and heaven commands.
Who points the clouds their course,
Whom winds and sea obey,
He shall direct thy wandering feet,
He shall prepare thy way.[1]

Marvelous to relate, on the third day of my arrest, a delegation from home was able to secure my release! But this was not the end of the matter, the Frenchmen of the administration started a conflict with the military court over its competence in permitting my release. With a heavy heart, I had to leave my parish without being able to give my parishioners an explanation.

After that, I had to start all over again in Darmstadt in an industrial parish of five thousand souls. I was first parochial assistant and then vicar; and everyone accepted me with great affection. In addition to my parish work I often sat up late into the night in the Trade Union building or in the Guild rooms debating with the proponents of that philosophy of life known as "Freethinking." People told me, "You personally could be our friend but your vicar preaches of the other world. We are fighting for a better world here below, and that is what separates us." I resisted the temptation to go into the working-class district and join the Social Democratic Party in order to share the whole life and struggles of a worker. It became clear to me that, as a Christian and a clergyman, I ought not to allow my civilized way of life (in the broad sense) to be flattened out by this leveling mania which is so often tyrannously applied to society. What I felt

1 Translation by J. Wesley.

I ought to do was to throw open the doors of my house with all its cultural advantages to the young workers so that they might share them. To a certain extent I was able to realize this project, especially in my youth work, because almost all of my parishioners were of the artisan or working classes.

My work expanded rapidly. For ten years I directed the Darmstadt branch of the "Evangelical Youth Society." In Hesse I founded a new youth league on the pattern of the *Jugendbewegung* (Youth Movement), and for two years, along with Professor Stählin, the leader of the Berneuchener liturgical movement, I was director of a vast youth league in Germany. This movement succeeded in winning a great many Evangelical Lutheran youths who had been strangers to church. The "youth movement" had everywhere affected the Christian youth associations. It seemed as though a new surge of life was passing through them and was revivifying everything. We hiked through half of Germany, camped in tents and sang with confidence, "We Are the Children of the New Age!" We believed in a new reality for mankind, springing from the strength of unspoiled youth. This unspoiled youth, we firmly believed, was capable of a new reverence for God, nature, history, our fellow men and God's image in our own souls. Such things as narrow middle-class ideas and conventional church-going were abhorred. Authority seemed to be based, not in the office, but only in the personal powers of the leaders. By his lectures and sermons Stählin shaped and led the youth both morally and religiously. I myself tried, particularly outside church, by making use of the first chapters of the Bible (Creation—Fall—Cain and Abel—Flood

—Tower of Babel), to lay the foundation of a Christian world-outlook.

This youth matured only gradually, and a concept of the limits of the human personality emerged slowly. New ideas about church and middle-class society were being formed and there was more understanding of the power of the Redemption. These young realized that the true leader must first learn to obey, and many of them are now in important positions in the church and in their professions. At that time they waged a brave struggle against the Hitler Youth until they were finally abandoned by their own Evangelical Church leaders.

Another valuable episode of my life was my participation in the Christian work for peace started by the French captain, E. Bach. This man gathered together Christians of all confessions and nations, who as *chevaliers de la paix* desired to live seriously in the peaceful spirit of Jesus. The movement is known today as the Christian Service for Peace. At one of its international conferences in Paris, I gave a lecture, in my capacity as a German Youth leader, with the object of awakening among the leading personalities there an understanding of the threatening dangers of unemployment to German youth; I also spoke of the necessity for a *rapprochement* between our two peoples which would spring from the Christian spirit. This, of course, was two years before Hitler's seizure of power!

True, I had not discovered by this route that ultimate reality which gives shape to the whole of life. This discovery was not made until God intervened in my life in a special manner.

One day, a lady from North Germany, Frau Margarete Dach, the wife of a senior judge in a lower court of justice, came to me to enroll her fifteen-year-old son in the confirmation course. After we had chatted for a while, I knew within me that here was the person I had been waiting for, one in whom the Christ of the Bible had really taken shape. Here at last I perceived the reality which supports, that fullness which gives life to all.

It is not easy to make the meaning of this statement clear to others who have not had a similar experience, but it must be attempted. Perhaps the significance of this event will reveal itself in the later story of my life.

A profound experience of faith caused this woman, when she had been mortally sick of a heart disease, to rise and be well in obedience to an inner prompting. She was convinced that Christ had intervened in her life, and was now aware of a new and profound existence in Him. A purely personal experience became for her an unprecedented grace.

But she did not stop at this personal experience. She saw beyond it to the saving will of God as it applies to all men. A door had opened for her into the fullness of God's kingdom. The key to this kingdom was faith, but it was a much more unconditional faith than Luther possessed, because it was a faith which was not only certain of personal redemption, but of the redemption of the whole world.

Thus she looked upon this gift as a definite commission imposed upon her to live, together with her whole house, in the spirit of this faith.

She was obediently attentive to the slightest sign from God. Everything she heard and did was at every moment spontaneous and fresh. She did nothing from mere selfish necessity, and, because of this, her mind was remarkably uncalculating. She lived always in the "now," the "today" of God's eternal present to His honor and glory. In every instance she first looked to God and only then, from Him to men, things, and events. She placed all her actions under His rule: all her speaking, reading, eating, walking, working, and resting, indeed, every handshake, everything down to the most trifling, the most commonplace action. Nothing any longer was a matter of indifference. There was nothing that should not be raised to the light, and bound up with God.

She also referred the most difficult situations to God, taking His point of view, trusting in everything to His love, and giving out in turn the radiance of this love. In this respect she acted like Peter, who first looked at Jesus and then was able to walk on the waves so long as he did not allow himself to be confused by the forbidding "apparent reality" of the raging water and the yawning deeps.

Thus, in this household, everything was constantly developing into a wonderful order and fullness, in which love permeated and awakened every living thing. A discipline reigned there which left nothing out of account. Anyone who wished to live there was obliged to sacrifice his "ego," his personal notions and wishes, and his trivial human standards of measurement; he had to submit himself entirely to the claims of God, to listen with reverence, and to be obedient in mind and action. Only thus was he set free for a new life as a child of God, detached from people and things in a spirit of having nothing and yet possessing all things in genuine profusion in their fullest power.

By the nature of her existence this lady convinced us again and again that such a state of living in union with Christ in the kingdom of God does really exist on earth. It made us aware that we need not wander through life always giving voluble expression to suffering, but rather we can achieve complete deliverance by the full acceptance and experience of pain.

Thus we went with her, as it were, from Good Friday when the Cross gives the death blow to "self," to Easter, which is the Resurrection and victory of the God-man and ourselves, since with Him we have all been revivified. We do not stop, as Luther did once, at the second article of belief in the Apostles' Creed—i.e., the Redemption—but we go back in a sense to the first article, the Creation. We ascend, if I may so express it, by faith to the heart of God, but from there we go *back* to His work. From the concept of God, the Creator, grows the reality which it was given to Luther to express so splendidly in his explanation of the first Commandment: ". . . and put my whole trust upon the pure, invisible, incomprehensible and only God, who made heaven and earth!"

I would like to emphasize that it was just in this way that we remained constantly aware of our own creaturehood, of our own incompleteness and inadequacy, and hence we felt it our duty to provide room in our hearts for God's work of grace and to let Him make use of us. As St. Paul has said (2 Cor. 3:5): "Not that we are sufficient of ourselves to think anything, as from ourselves, but our sufficiency is from God!"

In view of this, it is easy to see how important prayer was in that house. From it there grew that fine and sure instinct of the mother of the house, whom we affectionately called *"Dachmutter,"* because she seemed free from any influence of the Wicked One. Again and again she unmasked the subtle enemy. Our prayer was, above all, that of adoring praise. However, it was also insistent petition, and not a mere begging for the fulfillment of particular human wishes, but an introduction of all those needing help to the great stream of Christ's life in which all requests were put in Christ's hands. And it was often a request "in the name of Jesus" for His help in the battle against Satan. As a constant inspiration was the *Dachmutter's* prayer which never ceased.

In all our endeavors we sought to avoid "enthusiasms." There was no striving after the sensational. All we wished to do was to take the old Christian faith seriously, i.e., to literally live according to the words of Holy Scripture and its promises, which so many treat with so little respect.

Did not Jesus assure us that a faith "as small as a mustard seed" would have the power to move mountains; did He not say that all things were possible to him who believed? And what of the promise that the Father would give us anything that we asked in His name? Moreover, do we not recall that He said that His disciples would be given strength to tread upon serpents and scorpions, and upon all the power of the enemy, without being hurt? Did not the Apostle John rejoice in the experience of this authority: "Behold what love the Father has shown us. We were to be called the children of God, and we are. . . . Our faith is the victory which has overcome the world!'"?

This disciplined, loving, and joyous company of prayerful people was very like a religious order without a formulated rule. A little of the Church's true order was again perceptible in the form of the charism of a woman.

I have so far described what can serve as a paraphrase of those spiritual foundations which were to influence my life from that time on.

An example will show what strength can flow from such a spiritual renewal that grows by ever-new supplies of divine love, and even operates in the physical sphere. In 1925 I had undergone a series of four surgical operations which kept me in bed for half a year. A year later I found, as a result of the faith which the *Dachmutter* had been able to awaken in me, the courage to climb, without training but not without dizziness, the 12,000-foot high Gross-Venediger! And that was not my last attempt at mountain climbing.

It was also in the home of this marvelous woman that I met my future wife, Countess Bülow von Dennewitz from East Prussia, a great-grand-daughter of the famous Prussian field-marshal of the Wars of Liberation. She, too, was seeking that "fullness" which the good Lutheran home of her parents could not supply. An "accident," a late train, had led her to this house. From that moment her association with our *Dachmutter*, both in prayer and living, grew ever closer. This continued also after our marriage, for we regarded ourselves simply as instruments in the hands of God, and thus our new state brought blessings upon our group.

Our wedding ceremony was celebrated at Schloss Grün-hoff by Wilhelm Stählin who was at that time professor of theology in Münster and director with me of the youth league. Unfortunately we have had no children.

Meanwhile, conditions in Germany had altered radically as a result of the coming of National Socialism.

With what infallible clarity had our *Dachmutter* perceived this trend in 1932: "It is the devil," she suddenly remarked about this time. We owe it to her that we never for a single moment fell victims to the National Socialist seduction.

I remember distinctly that after the only discourse of Hitler I ever heard in person (at Darmstadt) on my way home I saw a meteor fall suddenly from the sky. I was reminded of the words of the prophet Isaias (14:12), "How art thou fallen from heaven, O Lucifer, who didst rise in the morning?"

After the Revolution how I should have loved to point out to those scorners of all human dignity the depths of their shame! But God did not impose upon me the task of waging open warfare. In preaching and in all other practical activities, I felt obliged to confine myself "to my Father's business." I tried to remain in the "middle," as upon a sort of storm-free rock of absolute belief in Christ's victory, so as not to be rent asunder by compromising or cooperating with the fascinating slogans. From this firm ground I was able to fight steadfastly for my Church. I could try to protect the entrances of the Church against the alien banners; I could fight against the falsification of the ecclesiastical elections ordered by Hitler; and I could, in particular, defend the church youth work. However, homes in the parish were broken into; we were twice besieged in our parish hall and parsonage. Then, suddenly, the newly-appointed "German Christian" provincial bishop, at the command of the Party, moved both my colleague (who had been in office at our church for nineteen years there) and myself, after four-and-a-half years there. This was our punishment.

The world upon which I had set my whole heart, the world in which I had been permitted to toil for twenty years as a parson dedicated to the youth of my country, seemed suddenly to be shattered into nothingness.

At the time *Dachmutter* told me, "If you fight for your right, you will waste your energies and be crushed. But if you accept your fate as coming not from man but from God you will lack nothing." And she was right. Since that day I have never missed what was taken from me, not even for a single moment.

Something really remarkable happened. Instead of being moved to the distant Odenwald, as was originally planned, I was moved to the leather-manufacturing town of Offenbach, not far from Frankfort. It was to this town, just three years earlier, that our friends from Darmstadt had moved, so that from 1934 onward we were able to fight together with renewed vigor for Christ against the satanic seduction of Nazism.

At my new post, which, however, was not put entirely in my charge until I had given evidence of my "good behavior" for six months, I soon found enjoyment in my work. I quickly found sympathy with the people there who were more or less thrown together from every part of Germany.

A majority of them seemed to sense the stream of divine love upon which I was borne. "Be loving with him all the same!" said *Dachmutter* to me once, as I was going out in a rather annoyed manner to a beggar who called periodically, always with the same story. And lo, the man forgot his intended request after I lent a sympathetic ear to his tale, and when he left me, both of us were enriched and happy.

My little town church had been Lutheran for two hundred years, before the unlucky "union" which had forced the Lutheran and "Reformed" together and brought about a leveling of their different confessional tenets.

Fortunately, I was able to restore the church, by many changes, to its former character, both within and without.

At the celebration of the Lord's Supper I took the liberty of making a number of changes, with the object of making this part of the service conform to some extent to the old Lutheran rite. Instead of ordinary white bread the faithful received round "hosts." Turning to the congregation, I raised both bread and wine and blessed the people with the Sign of the Cross, having an ardent hope that something had happened on the altar and that Christ was really present in the flesh. The communicants received both species, kneeling twelve at a time before the altar.

I treated baptism with quite a new seriousness, as a mysterious sacramental rite. It was a divine mystery and no longer a mere reception into the Church and an immersion into the spiritual society of Christ and His Redemption.

When I confirmed members of the Church, I adopted the less usual formula: "Receive the Holy Ghost," not the more usual "The Holy Ghost be with you," but I always bore in my heart the fearful question, "Have my hands really the power to confer the Spirit?" Also before their first communion I always gave them the choice of going to confession or not. I still remember, as though it happened today, how a child confided to me a really grave sin, and I remember that I asked myself with a feeling of terror, "Have I really the authority to say, 'I absolve thee'?"

Often in the service I prayed the splendid *Gloria in Excelsis Deo* and gradually I was able to introduce one beautiful liturgical prayer after another. Later, during the war, evening devotions of a purely liturgical character were adopted.

A colleague who was strictly of "united" observance denounced me to the provost at Darmstadt on account of these novelties which were introduced, of course, on my own authority, although not without the consent of the church authorities. Fortunately, the provost did not regard this grave period of national struggle as a suitable time for such arguments *intra muros*.

On the other hand the *Dachmutter* gave me every assistance, especially in our lively theological struggles to reach the depths of truth. Moreover, I obtained my parish assistant from her house, a fine lady who worked for eight years at my side. A secondary-school mistress became Church Superintendent, while other ladies helped with the Children's Service or sang in the choir, and we all felt we were building a Church in the spirit of Luther! In the house of our *Dachmutter* there developed, moreover, a life which grew more animated day by day. She was like a magnet to people who were seeking life. Healthy people and sick ones often came from considerable distances, and she won many to her belief in that ineffable grace of being the children of God.

With what depth and conscientiousness did *Dachmutter* harmonize the piety of our times with that of the past. She sat up late into the night praying over her Bible, and spent her days helping whomever she could. However, she did not feel called upon to speak with everyone, because here too she remained at the divine bidding. She believed she might not pray for everyone, and, in particular, not for that man who as the "Anti-Christ" was trying to destroy Christ's kingdom. At the time, that man's name was never mentioned in the house, so that it was possible for a child to return home after his first day at school and ask: "Say, is there really a man named Adolf Hitler?"

The "Stapo" had indeed long nursed a suspicion concerning us, but they could discover nothing dangerous when they paid us a visit. How could the members of the Gestapo inflated as they were with military power guess that in this house, by day and night, and in the daily domestic devotions of *Dachmutter,* Christ's victory was extolled beyond the might of their regime; that by this means a spiritual power was generated which they could not lay their hands on in any case? God alone knows to what extent this flood of prayer helped to prevent more dreadful occurrences.

It was at this grave time that the *Dachmutter* used to go almost daily with my wife, and other ladies who joined them in their prayers, to the Blessed Mother's altar in St. Paul's Catholic Church to storm the "Queen of Peace" with their ardent petitions. From her earliest childhood *Dachmutter* had a tender affection for the glorious Virgin, the Mother of God. She loved to visit her little chapels during the Holy Days because these had a unique atmosphere of prayer which she found especially attractive.

I, too, found myself nearer to the Catholic Church in these very dangerous times. In fact the two religions, Lutheran and Catholic, depended upon one another in their defensive struggle against the man who threatened the very basis of their faiths. This closer association began in our little efforts to help one another. Thus the assistant of the nearby parish of St. Paul's often gave me a lift to school in his car. We were delighted to see the wry faces of the National Socialist teachers when they saw the representatives of the two "Christianities" get out of the car peacefully together as representatives of a united "black power." The pastor, too, was on the best of terms with me. Whenever one of us returned from an involuntary absence, necessitated by the demands of the current officialdom, it was always the other who was the first to congratulate him. As a matter of fact, I was never a prey to those well-known prejudices against Catholics. It always struck me as a sign of weakness when, for example, the "Evangelical League" appeared to draw its life from its opposition to the Catholic Church. Naturally this organization had long since excluded me from its ranks.

Something surprising happened in Protestant circles at this period. Evangelical believers sighed with relief when men suddenly appeared who, without concern for their personal safety, stood up against the rape of the Church by the National Socialist State. Consider the risks taken by, for example, Martin Niemöller in gathering into his *Pfarrernot-*

bund (Pastors' Emergency League) all the clergy who were opposed to applying the "Arian" pronouncements either to themselves or the faithful. In those days we had something like a "Church" again.

The silent work carried on by faithful theologians after the First World War was now bearing its first fruits, even if these were not yet recognizable. Consider the developments in the field of New Testament research, the new realizations of the meaning of such terms as "office," "sacrament" and "Church"! Professor Schlier was one of the pioneers in the studies. Consider the progress in the history of dogmas and of the Church (e.g. Peter in Rome!) and in liturgical matters. The liturgical revival is well-known. This reawakened the sense of worship and raised the sacred rites from their Cinderella-like role of being mere accessories of divine service to their royal position in the real "service of God." The revival was largely brought about by Stählin's foundation of the Brotherhood of St. Michael [2] and his introduction of the German Mass, and also by the "High Church" movement of Professor Heiler. This revival was intensified by the "Lutheran Liturgical Conference" (for the renewal of the liturgy within the Lutheran Church) which initiated much extremely careful research not confined merely to the teachings of Luther but reached back to the most primitive forms of Church service.

Many of these things developed as a result of the daily challenge to the basic truths of Christianity. Confronted by

---

[2] Derived from the Berneuchener Movement, the Brotherhood of Saint Michael works for a spiritual revival of the Protestant Church through a unity of teaching and divine service.

the "New Paganism" of Reichsbischof Müller and his "German Christians," people were now obliged to ask themselves, "What are the basic principles of our faith?" A tree encompassed by a storm sends its roots more deeply into the soil.

It was thus that people returned to their belief in Christ as the Son of God. At an undenominational Protestant synod in Barmen, nineteen out of twenty-eight provincial Churches, wonderfully united, rose above their confessional differences against the "German Christian" heresy and the totalitarian claims of the National Socialist State. They professed their faith in the undivided dominion of Jesus Christ and in the Word of God, beside which they did not recognize as God's revelation "other events and forces, figures and truths." Thus they laid some claim to the "teaching office."

In this fight against the efforts of the State to create a German Christian State Church, people were forced to give serious thought to a really genuine Church order. The pastoral office finally came to life as new emergency organs of direction were created in the establishment of the National Council of Brethren, the Confessional Synod, and the Provisional Church Administration. Use was made of the "power of the keys" when, at the second, the Dahlem, synod, Reichsbishop Müller was anathematized, and those present dissociated themselves from the neutrals. Thus in the bitter struggle, it was possible to see how necessary it is for the Church to have an order, a hierarchy which preserves, protects, and mediates the faith. If only at a later date this realization had continued to grow!

In Offenbach and Frankfort, too, it was amazing to see

how gladly people flocked to these councils. Once again there were some, even among the Evangelical Christians, who were prepared to risk their lives for their faith. The old fighting songs of the Reformation period were lustily sung again. I still remember how I had to accompany banished speakers who were being taken by the Gestapo to the borders of the province near Frankfort, yet in spite of this, new speakers continued to appear, and one leapt into the struggle however and whenever one could. Still, one asked oneself if anything new was really going to come of this.

My town parish, too, joined what was now called the Confessing Church, and our parson gradually came to a position of leadership. Previously I had never bothered myself with Church politics. The haggling of the three schools of thought in the Church (orthodox, middle, and liberal) to determine the occupation of key positions was distasteful to me. But now the very life and existence of the Christian Church was at stake. From 1938 onward I was a member of the *Landesbruderrat* in Frankfort. This was an underground Church government in provinces which, like Nassau-Hesse, had an imposed "German-Christian" regime. It even maintained its own secret theological seminary. Many are the sessions and synods in which I took part at that time. Members wanted to support their whole claim upon the "Word," and the will of God was thought to be revealed in the decision of the elected members. But this did not give a real clarity and decision to our actions: I can still hear one of the theological teachers sighing, "If only we really were the 'Church.'"

At first our friends joyfully shared in these signs of life in a Church which at last seemed to be waking up. This change in the Evangelical Church was noticed with astonishment, even in the Catholic Church, which was glad to have allies in its struggle. The Una-Sancta discussions which took place later were first made possible by this change. Of course, there were soon reactions from the government. Although the State did not dare to prohibit the Confessing Church, it checked her activity in every direction, with a corresponding increase in its acts of violence. The year 1937 was one of arrests. To give just one authentic example, I have before me a report from the National Council of Brethren and the Provisional Church Administration of the Confessing Church in Germany of the Church's position on November 24, 1937: forty arrests, twenty-seven suspensions from office, thirty-one prohibitions from speaking, forty-one expulsions to another area, and thirty-eight rustications of students at the universities, not to mention the fact that Niemöller had been in prison since July 1, 1937.

But the Reich Church Minister also tried maneuvers that were more clever by means of his "Church Committees," the object of which were to bring together the State-directed "German-Christian" Church authorities and the clergy of the Confessing Church. He hoped thus to level out their differing tenets and to end the former conflict by compromise.

Much more dangerous to the life of the "Confessing Church" were the internal struggles which broke out within her own ranks. It is true that the Barmen Synod had united Lutherans and the Reformed Churches in a common witness in opposition to the "German Christians." But those deeply-rooted differences of belief (e.g., in regard to Church government and the doctrine of the Lord's Supper) were already apparent at the Oeynhausen Synod. The relations between the Lutheran Council and the "Confessing Church," to which Karl Barth was giving an increasingly distinct "Reformed" character, became extremely tense. It was found impossible to clear up these differences of belief even after several discussions at Frankfort on the subject of the Lord's Supper.

The old ecclesiastical regimes of those provincial Churches, which were still more closely bound to tradition, were in a sort of natural opposition to the more independent National Council of Brethren, especially to those in the regions devastated by war.

Finally, the Confessing Church suffered, in spite of her newly-acquired religious experience and realization, because among her clergy there were still a large number of adherents of the old theological liberalism. (Bultmann might be mentioned here, because even though he is quite an extreme example, he is one that is nevertheless especially relevant.) It was about this time that our *Dachmutter* sent her brother-in-law, Professor Spira, a teacher of English philology at Königsberg in addition to being a well-read theologian, and myself, together with certain Berlin friends belonging to the former Niemöller circle, to contact prominent representatives of the various Church groups. Our mission was intended to unite at least all those who acknowledged "Jesus Christ, the Son of God," but nothing came of it. The serious call had no visible result. We even went to Catholic bishops to make our desires known, and our reception there was very sympathetic.

Somewhat about the same time, Wurm, the bishop of the

Württemberg province, was trying to unite in his *Einigungs-werk* the clergy of the Confessing Church and that of the so-called "middle Church" (half-way between the Confessing Church and the "German Christians").

We succeeded in gathering together on January 25, 1939, in St. Matthew's Church at Frankfort, about eight hundred clergy from Nassau-Hesse. There the provincial bishop, Dietrich, who had been cold-shouldered by the Nazis for a long time, and with whom I had carried out negotiations on behalf of the National Council of Brethren, openly recanted his actions of the first years. With this amalgamation, however, no true inner theological unity was achieved, and the mistrust born in the period of early struggle was not yet dead. Thus, even this merger was not attended with any very fruitful results.

The persecution and subsequent annihilation of the Jews, which began with the burning of the synagogues in 1938, cast a deep shadow upon my life. In the pulpit I openly denounced these brutalities which so blatantly disregarded the Fifth Commandment. I declared that these acts were not made any less grave, but were rather revealed in their true nature, by the fact that the two stone tablets of the Law had actually been chiseled out of the synagogue in Offenbach! As a result of my denunciations, one anxious churchwarden immediately resigned his office.

In spite of those things, I remained under God's protecting mantle. Of course, I had to put up with all sorts of irritations. At that time the clergy were put out of the schools and our sermons were delivered to congregations interspersed with government agents. But we helped one another. I recall preparing duplicates of many of the notices of the Confessing Church so that if I were arrested a church-warden of the parish circle could still read them out. Many of the addresses of Bishop Count Galen or Bishop Wurm against the breaches of the law, euthanasia, sterilization, and the mass gassings were secretly copied and surreptitiously passed on. Sunday after Sunday I prayed during our services for Niemöller as the representative of all the other prisoners.

It was at that time the misfortune of the Jews went to my very marrow. How little it was we could do for them. We clergy, it is true, refused to give up the names of bap-tized Jews from the church registers, and I remember that I allowed them to go to the Lord's Supper wearing the Jew-ish star. But it is not hard to imagine how wretched was the minister's position when a Jewess he had baptized knelt before him with a fellow victim and implored, "Help us!" All I could give the poor creatures other than words of consolation were little crucifixes, tracts with passages from the Bible and some fitting hymns to accompany them to Auschwitz. (Also, I did at least secretly bury other Christian Jews, whom I had known in Darmstadt, in the Jewish ceme-tery, or in the public cemetery in Frankfort.) God spared me, through a journey I had to make in 1943, the necessity of watching the final exodus of these poor, unfortunate crea-tures.

At that time *Dachmutter,* who felt desolate because of these events and who had faithfully prayed that our cities should be preserved from bombing attacks, declared, "God told the Jews, in spite of their apostasy, 'Anyone who touches you, touches the apple of My eye.' Hence, I no longer feel

any obligation to pray for the towns, like Offenbach and
Frankfort, that have driven out the Jews."

In the years 1937 and 1938, my wife and I went hiking
in the Spessart during my holidays. Our destination one day
was Rothenfels, a castle now used as a youth hostel for the
Quickborners,[3] whom we had always greatly valued as allies
during our days in the Youth Movement. We also called at
the Löwenstein hunting lodge, Karlshöhe, and, to our astonishment, met there a number of theology students from St.
George's Seminary in Frankfort-Oberrad who were playing
ball in their black soutanes. This was a sight to which we
were unaccustomed. When we asked directions for our future route, we were led "by chance" to the host of the entire
group, their fellow student at St. George's, Prince Franz zu
Löwenstein. He not only gave us directions but went along
with us for some distance. Near a charcoal-burner's kiln we
got into a deep conversation which, shortly afterward, when
we reached a little spring, developed into a discussion of the
sixth chapter of St. John and its personal or sacramental
meaning. The result of this was that the prince often came
from Oberrad to visit us in Offenbach, and, eventually became one of the close friends of our circle. A year later, after
he was ordained, the prince invited the Evangelical parson
of Offenbach and his wife to be guests at his first Mass in
Schloss Heubach. We were all deeply impressed when the
prince said how thankful he was that not one member of his
numerous family was absent from the Communion rail that
morning. Later on, in the last letter he wrote before his

[3] Members of the Quickborn Catholic Youth Movement which started
in 1909.

death, he congratulated me upon the occasion of my first Mass.

And this man's son, who was the Jesuit, Father Franz, spent much of his valuable spare time among us in the years that followed, leading many into the Catholic Church. I was one of the last he received into the Church in the Cathedral of Mainz. Afterward, he was my sponsor at confirmation.

It may have been about the year 1938 or 1939 that *Dachmutter* got hold of the Catholic Missal published by Schott. After this she saw more deeply into the meaning of the Holy Mass which she and other members of the household now attended in St. Paul's Church. From the prayer of the Mass the complete reality of Christ's presence in the Holy Eucharist became clear to them, as it did not in my Lutheran Lord's Supper in the town church. Illustrated lectures at St. Mary's school helped to explain to them the liturgy of the Holy Mass. With these aids they slowly prayed themselves into the Catholic Church. It would be impossible to count the number of prayers for intercession that were said. The prayers were both numerous and fervent that went up to God in *Dachmutter's* house after the death of Pope Pius XI, in February, 1939, for the election of the new "Father of Christendom." And when Pius XII was elected, I begged my Evangelical parishoners during divine service to pray earnestly for him in his office of Christendom's chief pastor.

Shortly after this the war came. In many ways the political oppression was lightened, but now everything was subject to the laws of war and anything could happen. Our young Confessing-Church theologians were rigorously conscripted or expelled from the administrative district of Wiesbaden. The leading men of the National Council of Brethren in Frankfort disappeared to the Front one after the other or else they were imprisoned. Other members were forbidden to voice their sentiments by threats of expulsion. In 1940, therefore, I had to take over the leadership of the Council of Brethren. During this year I took part in the examination and ordination of about thirty young Confessing-Church theologians trained in Frankfort. These activities took place "abroad," so to speak, far from the grip of the Gestapo in Hesse. These young men, furthermore, had to find positions in churches in other provinces. Among these young theologians was Otto Melchers of Bremen who had come into *Dachmutter*'s house through the family of my brother. Melchers was later on a curate of mine for a time.

His examination thesis presented at Frankfort dealt with Luther's work, *On the Turks*. This topic was discussed with animation in *Dachmutter*'s house, and it directed the thoughts of the entire circle toward the ultimate theological concepts. They now began to read Luther's writings. The confessional statements of the Reformation and Karl Barth's *Theological Existence Today* and also his *Nein* were studied. Karl Barth had turned Evangelical theology right back to the absolute theonomy of Luther and to Asmussen's *Sola fide*. Other works we read were certain writings by Lackmann, Karl Barth's *Credo*, Vischer's *Christuszeugnis im alten Testament*, Bonhoeffer's *Nachfolge*, the New Testament theology of Ethelbert Stauffer, the dogmatic theology of Schmaus, and many other books. Moreover, we became acquainted with such great Catholic saints as Thérèse of Lisieux, whose character we found so congenial, St. Bridget of Sweden, and the great

Teresa of Ávila, whose personality had so much in common with that of our *Dachmutter*.

It was about that time, too, that Professor Joseph Lortz published his book on the Reformation in Germany, which was a pioneering work with the intention of reuniting the separated Christian sects under one basic creed. And these ideas were brought even more to the public attention by the professor's own lectures. A Catholic would probably find it difficult to imagine the immense effect this had on Evangelical churchmen. With profound pleasure they encountered here a Catholic scholar who with genuine brotherly feeling and courageous justice was striving to reassess and re-present in an unbiased manner the phenomenon of Luther. This attitude in itself meant a contact between the different denominations which would never be lost.

With this effective stimulation, the *Una Sancta* conversations, which were held in various places at that time, became more animated. I myself took part in a typical inter-denominational discussion in Bonn, at which, besides myself, Professor Spira, Pastor Asmussen and Pastor Kloppenburg of Oldenburg were present. It is pertinent that I mention at this point, even if it is somewhat anticipatory, that there was a great gathering of representatives of many German *Una Sancta* groups, especially those of the Confessing Church, which took place in Berlin in 1942. At this conference, I was the delegate of the Provincial Brotherhood Council. I remember that in the evening many of us went down to a subterranean community hall, where a secret Church meeting was held for the whole of Germany. In the afternoon of the same day I had a long and delightful audience with

Count Preysing, the bishop of Berlin, who spoke of his difficult and dangerous work. I was able to tell him of *Dachmutter* and our movement and received his blessing at my departure.

On holiday in the Tyrol with *Dachmutter,* her husband (who was an excellent painter), and my wife, we met Professor Adam of Tübingen several times. I was at last able to be present at the celebration of Mass in the little Volderwildbader chapel. I was impressed by this priest's holiness, and his services had a very profound effect upon me. With him I scrambled about the mountains and we discussed in a very spontaneous way the manifold aspects of the doctrine of grace. Guardini's beautiful book, *The Lord,* the life of St. Hildegard, and Katherine Emmerich's very moving account of the passion of Christ provided some weighty holiday reading.

I recall that one day in Innsbruck we prayed for a long time before Cranach's wonder-working image of the Madonna in the parish church of Sankt-Jakob's; it was the day on which the first enemy aircraft flew over this city. I sensed the power which flows from a picture of this sort, hallowed as it is by the prayers of so many. We were told that it was because of the prayers offered before this image that Innsbruck by Mary's intercession was saved from destruction in the Thirty Years' War, and that Tyrol remained Catholic and avoided religious divisions by reforming itself. Since that time this Innsbruck Madonna has remained especially intimate and meaningful for me. In the spring of 1953, while on my pilgrimage to Rome, I found great pleasure in celebrating Holy Mass before this image.

Of very great significance, considering all the seeking and questioning that was going on in our circle in 1940, was our meeting with Dr. Schmitt who at that time was assistant at St. Paul's in Offenbach, but who later became professor of theology in Mainz. His important sermons and lectures opened up the beliefs of the Catholic world to many. Scarcely any Sunday passed in which he did not take part in our afternoon theological discussions. He helped us considerably by clarifying many points. With great understanding and warm affection he appreciated the religious concerns of our circle. And so, one day, *Dachmutter* was able to announce, "Starting today we will have no further controversial discussions. We must now listen to what the Church has to say."

Dr. Schmitt was also very helpful to us in the small liturgical conference that had been arranged by the Provincial Council of Brethren, and which our *Dachmutter* and my wife finally attended in my house. At monthly meetings we worked through all the parts of the Mass in one year.

Nevertheless, there were still things I found difficult to comprehend. It was very hard for me to understand at that time the co-existence of justice and love in the heart of God, especially in connection with the authority in the kingdom of Christ. And only slowly did I become aware of the organic and symbolic signification of the liturgy. Yet these matters seemed to be treated as of little importance in Article 7 of the Augsburg Confession, "And it is not essential to the true unity of the Christian Church that uniform ceremonies, introduced by man, should everywhere be held."

One day Dr. Schmitt brought a guest to *Dachmutter*'s

house. This was the bishop of Mainz, Albert Stohr. As a result of his visit, which occupied much more time than he had anticipated, the bishop was deeply impressed by the spirit which pervaded this house, and he has remained our fatherly and understanding protector to this day. Since 1946 we have attended the so-called "Braunshardter Conference" with him twice a year. This conference was founded by the archbishop of Paderborn who was introduced to us by the bishop of Mainz with the object of intensifying the spiritual life and faith of both parties in the spirit of our *Dachmutter*. And through all these spiritual preparations, final decisions were slowly being arrived at in our circle. Eventually many of us were guided into the Church by Dr. Schmitt, who received *Dachmutter* and her husband, and later, my wife, in the Cathedral of Mainz.

In our struggle toward belief and our desire for complete deliverance from the powers of darkness, we recognized a single reality, Christ the God-man, who was truly both God and man and, therefore, the embodiment of all true being. Because of this realization, we began to approach even more intimately the very foundations of Christian existence. Then, to our astonishment, we discovered a completely consistent faith resting upon the foundations of the One, Holy Church. Once we had seen that the operation of Christ's Sacred Humanity signified the sanctification of humble labor, everyday events, and all the objects of the material universe, we knew that Christ accomplishes man's justification not only in heaven as Luther thought, but here on earth. And this process is not purely "spiritual" but concrete and tangible, and, hence, we learned to recognize the sacraments of the Church as the outward sources of invisible grace and pledges of a redemption already begun.

The *one* Church was thus recognized as the body of the *one* "man," Jesus Christ who was also God. In the course of these years, many of us from the most varied walks of life found our way to her abundance, the fulfillment of all that God had shown us along the way, the way that our *Dachmutter* had taken before any of us. All of these "pilgrims" believed, with her, that they had returned along the path of Luther, and that in doing so they had witnessed the unity of the Church, and, therefore, they dedicated themselves to the reunion of Christians, feeling it to be a command from God that was especially applicable to our times. And what about myself?

I could participate in all this only to a limited extent because I had, after all, a parish of four to five thousand souls, work in the Frankfort Provincial Council of Brethren, the spiritual care of a home for the aged, and, in 1940, similar duties in the Offenbach military hospital as well. This latter concern often kept me busy until late at night, because it was only after all the orderlies had gone that pastoral discussions were at last really possible. As can readily be imagined, there was no time then for reading and serious study, and any participation in Catholic worship was clearly out of the question.

But God did provide a short interval in a rather unexpected way. I had argued with a soldier in the hospital that a true Christian may not have any sentiments of hate, and I thus challenged the "hate speeches" made by Herr Fritsche on the radio. I was reported to the authorities, denounced, and interrogated for five hours, and then I was charged with demoralizing the army! In the end, I was taken into protective custody for three weeks and threatened with a concentration camp. I was taken to the same county court prison in which I had shortly before held services. Now, at last, there was time to read books. I read Karl Adam's *Spirit of Catholicism,* Lortz' work on the Reformation in Germany, a study of St. Augustine and other works. When this time of blessing was at an end and my wife came to take me home, I was almost sad.

From that time on, the services in my church were not so well attended, and there were many who no longer dared to speak to me on the street. Interruptions and disturbances of services and confirmation classes increased.

I recall that at this time, the ladies of the Women's Union of the town parish came to see my wife and called her to account because they had observed that she spent a great deal of time praying in the Catholic church of St. Paul, even on Sundays after the service. They said, "It is inadmissible that the wife of the Evangelical pastor should go to a Catholic church." My wife answered, "I can understand your surprise, but I do not do it of my own volition, or because I necessarily want it that way, but because I know it is God's will and I can pray better there. And, also, the Evangelical churches are sometimes closed." Thereupon a lady stood up and said, "If God has bidden our pastor's wife to act in this manner, we can do nothing else but back up her prayers."

In the summer of 1941 I had to go to Bad Brückenau for lengthy treatment, and there I had opportunities to visit a Catholic church. I enjoyed the courageous, carefree, and dogmatically profound sermons of the chaplain, Dr. Sauer. We had many theological discussions and he tried to clarify for me the Catholic doctrine of the condition of man before the Fall. With the help of Möhler's *Symbolik,* he showed me how the consequences that Luther drew from the Fall differed from those of the Catholic Church. Thus I began to understand better some of the differing views on the doctrine of justification.

The war grew more and more grave, and even when I was in prison I heard the first French aircraft droning over our town. The building shook when the anti-aircraft guns on the nearby railway fired, and there was no air raid shelter for prisoners. Yet, this was only a presage of the frightful bombing attacks of the years that followed. How often did I hurry in the night from one sickbed to another, through the smoking streets after an attack, to see whether those committed to my care were still living, and to console them with my prayers. I remember that I was sustained once again by the splendid words of Luther's version of the Bible, or the consoling hymns of the church, especially the one written by Paul Gerhardt.

Finally, we had to suffer from the raging fires like all the rest, possibly to show our communion with the poor, who like us were members of Christ's body and had to endure God's fearful judgment upon our nation. On October 4, 1943, *Dachmutter's* house was burned down. We had thought that this house was under some sort of special protection and we were horrified, but not so our *Dachmutter.* She said, "This then is Thy will, dear Lord? 'My soul magnifies the Lord and my spirit rejoices in God, my Saviour.'"

Nevertheless, we were able to save quite a number of things, for helpers appeared from near and far as though some secret understanding existed. Our group immediately found refuge in a new house in Kronberg which God in His providence had provided for them, so that their good work could continue to be carried on from there. Thus, by accepting God's will, they received back from Him all that was necessary. The memory of this spirit of humble submission gave strength to my wife and myself when we suffered the same fate. Our own house was burned to ashes on December 20th of the same year, and everything we owned went with it. We were now travelers with light luggage once again. My wife found refuge at Kronberg and I lived a bachelor's life once more in the former curate's rooms in Offenbach. My ministry was certainly made very difficult by the frequent sound of air raid sirens which drove our unfortunate people again and again into the shelters.

The parish house was partially burned, and we finally had to experience the loss of the beautiful town church which went up in flames the night before confirmation services. These had to be held then in a half-ruined parish hall in which we had erected the altar saved from the burning church. A mere handful of dirty children who had emerged from the bomb shelters was present, while the delayed-action bombs were still exploding outside.

Since, during all this time, many of my parishoners lost their homes or had escaped from the town in their fear, my parish dwindled to a tiny group and my work was a mere shadow of what it was formerly. My superiors, therefore, moved me to the large country parish of Rossdorf near Darmstadt which was still intact and whose pastor had been called to the Front. It was with a heavy heart that I left my own charges who were in danger. Here, too, as formerly in Darmstadt, our *Dachmutter*'s guidance decided the issue and I went willingly. Once again obedience to a sign from God brought me blessing, and there is no doubt that my later course would have been quite different if this had not happened.

The two years at Rossdorf, which were the last two years of my ministry as a pastor, were delightful. My spiritual relationship with my parish was most intimate and rewarding. I introduced an older form of Eucharistic service with the Kyrie and Gloria, a liturgical restoration made by the Lutherans of the Confessing Church in the Rhineland. Moreover, I placed candles and flowers upon the altar, because this seemed appropriate since Rossdorf, too, was an old Lutheran parish. I also allowed the Catholic community to celebrate Holy Mass in our church, and I attended the first celebration from the door of the sacristy.

Besides this, I was grateful to be able to keep in touch with my parish in Offenbach, and did so fairly easily until the trains ceased to run altogether. I then had to be constantly changing my sleeping quarters because there was a danger that the Nazis might arrest me during the night. I recall that I made my last journey back in a truck just before the Americans entered Rossdorf after a victorious bombardment and a brief skirmish. Because I was a pastor, I received a passport very soon and then went immediately to Darmstadt with three colleagues of the Confessing Church in order to relegate to the past the last remnants of the

"German Christian" regime. With several ministers from the "Middle Church" we formed a new "Provisional Church Administration" for the Church in the province of Hesse.

The first meetings of this organization took place in my Rossdorf parish house. One day the bishop of Mainz appeared, and I was very glad because I had sought him in vain in his city in order to consult with him about our discussions. He came to my parsonage from Darmstadt, where he was then living. We instituted what we called a "Conference of Understanding" between the two church governments, so as to present a common front to the new State and to clear away all conflicts which might arise between the two Churches. This Conference lasted for four years and the proceedings ran very smoothly. The bishop of Mainz was always present and, later on, so was the bishop of Limburg. In addition, there were all the Evangelical Church executives of Hesse-Nassau and the present ministerial councilor, Professor Spira who was then liaison officer for the government. However, the political utterances of the president of the Provincial Church of Hesse, Niemöller, finally brought this cooperation to an end.

In the Provincial Church Administration, it was my business among other things to report on "secondary schools," and on "relations with the Catholic Church" as I did formerly in the Provincial Council of Brethren. At that time I succeeded in reopening the former *Realgymnasium* in Laubach as a church school that took boarders, and in opening a church Realgymnasium in Rimhorn, and thus I managed to strengthen Christian influence in our province.

In the meantime, the pastor of Rossdorf had returned

from the army. Before leaving the city, we placed a tall cross on the Rehberg. Appropriately, this was about the time of the Feast of the Ascension. The cross bore the inscriptions: "In memory of the wonderful deliverance of Rossdorf in World War II" and in large letters in the crossbeam "Christ is the victor!"

After a short period of activity in office in Darmstadt, I was appointed chief counselor to the Ecclesiastical Commission of the Hesse Ministry of Religion on November 1, 1946. My particular sphere of work was ecclesiastical education as a whole. This position made it possible for me to make many contacts with the various Christian denominations. I was able to influence the minister of education's new school decree substantially and to make sure that it contained adequate provision for religious instruction in all types of schools. This was something new for the technical schools, and I had to fight hard in the school committee of the province to win acceptance for this.

Commissioned by the Branch of Religious Affairs of the American military government, I prepared two voluminous works: one on the position of the Christian press prior to 1933 and in July, 1948, the other on the church school in Hesse prior to 1933. My association with these American gentlemen, who both were pious Catholic Christians, was most agreeable.

The "Conference of Understanding," that had been so wantonly dissolved for political reasons, was restored in a new form. The military government assembled the representatives of all the Christian Churches, including those of the diocese of Fulda, and there were monthly consultations with the Branch of Religious Affairs, with representatives of the Ministry of Religion, and among the members themselves. This system was continued in the Hesse Ministry of Religion after the termination of the American civil administration, and it has done much good.

After two years, the activities of this Conference were greatly diminished, and upon completing my tasks, therefore, I resigned at the age of sixty-eight.

At the very beginning of my activity as an official, God called our *Dachmutter* to Himself and, for the moment, everything seemed very dark to us. But once again God had ordained quite otherwise than we expected, and we learned to understand how her illness and death were a singular victory which truly revealed Christ's glory. Uniting herself to the strength of the beloved Mother of God she was raised above her sufferings while she waited upon the royal road of faith, ready to live to the last in God's service or to die, as He willed. But the help of her manifold graces was not taken from us at her death. Her home has continued to be a place of ineffable blessing even to the present time. I was very soon able to feel in my own life the wonderful effects of her guidance.

About this time it came to my attention that the Holy Father had considered conferring the sacrament of ordination upon married Evangelical pastors who had devoted themselves to the cause of Christian reunification and who were fitted to continue working for it; the ordination was not to interfere with the state of the existing sacramental marriage. I was at first terribly frightened. It seemed to me that the ground was sinking under my feet. However, at a later date this offer became the firm foundation of my life because, with our bishop, I saw in it the will of God.

But, of course, the first thing I had to think about was becoming a Catholic, and, after my work in the Ministry of Religion was terminated, I had time for study at last. A thorough and protracted theological examination was to be expected and I plunged deeply into dogmatic theology but also worked through the Reformation writings that Luther completed after 1520. I was guided by Professor Lortz and one of his colleagues put me in touch with Holl, Köstlin, and others. I read the Augsburg Confession after I finished Asmussen's book, *Warum noch lutherische Kirche*. Sometimes I was able to pursue my studies in the Catholic rectory in Presberg, a village high up in the Taunus, where the pastor, Father Wagenbach, was always on hand to answer my questions. I was also able to learn from him what was required of a good Catholic priest.

All the things that had been revealed to me and awakened in me during the previous years now came to maturity. Many points, it is true, had to be investigated all over again. I cannot describe all this in detail here, but there is just one thing in particular I should like to mention. I found great pleasure in meditating on the Blessed Trinity. Because of Luther and my former theological teacher, Hermann, I had become accustomed to rejecting the assistance of philosophy in dogmatic theology. I now saw how well the philosophico-theological system of the wise and devout St. Thomas Aquinas could sharpen our understanding of both the inexhaustible fullness of God as the *esse per se subsistens* and of the mystery of the gradation of beings whose limited existence depends on Him. Consequently, I became more fully aware of the meaning of that love which circulates within the Trinity, and into which, we, too, are drawn.

Christology, too, gave my faith in the divine sonship of Christ its first real depth. It is only that person who understands the Incarnation of the Word to some degree who can properly comprehend the significance of the sacraments. Nowadays even Evangelical churchmen are beginning to understand what the Swabian Evangelical theologian, Oetinger, meant by corporeality, i.e., that God manifests Himself to us through corporeal means. How necessary is the supporting objectivity of the sacraments to those who formerly lived upon purely personal piety! The Evangelical professor, Sommerlath, once pointed out at the Frankfort discussions on the Lord's Supper that man not only meets God at the summit of his own personality, in consciousness, but he is connected with God, unconsciously, by the very fact of his creaturely existence.

By thinking about these things, the center of gravity finally shifted in me from the merely personal to the objective, and so I gained an ever-deeper understanding of the essential objectivity of sacramental action. At the same time I was also able to grasp the objectivity of divine worship. I saw it as something more than merely personal edification, as the adoration and glorification of the Holy Trinity in harmony with the worship of the angels and the saints. The center of gravity was shifting more and more from the ego to the heart of God.

Indeed, I felt the gate of heaven itself opening wider above me as God's holy Mother with all the angels and saints became genuinely real to me as fellow combatants and allies of the Church Militant here below. I knew that the universality of experience was definitely far beyond all the limits that Kant drew for it. It was not difficult to be at home in heaven either, because we knew our *Dachmutter* was there in any case. We had discovered through her some knowledge of the nature and love of the Blessed Mother of God even here on earth, and we were sure that she was interceding for us.

I found it very difficult to grasp the meaning of sanctifying grace as *gratia creata* until, one day, seeing the rich layer of earth lying upon rocky ground, nature afforded me a sudden illumination. This sense image was revealed to me as a symbol of the action of grace on the soul. I perceived grace to be the leaven that permeates and enriches the nature of man, a condition, which, if accepted, results in total transformation. It is the "wedding garment" that permits us to take part in the life of God Himself so that we might return to Him the abundant fruits we have gathered as His co-redeemers.

However, the thing that made more impression on me than any doctrinal teaching was the reverent attitude of holy priests at the altar. This helped me to take the last step of faith, belief in the reality of substantial change in the Holy Eucharist at the Consecration of the Mass.

By a purely intellectual approach to the Church it is likely that a true Protestant, or anyone who sincerely seeks truth, will still have some doubts as to the scriptural warrant for this or that doctrine. On this point, Father zu Löwenstein once gave me some very helpful encouragement. He said,

"You will never reach complete clarity that way. You must first take to heart the fact that the Church herself is a sacrament, the Body of the everliving Christ, who demands and claims *you*." Yes, this is the salient factor, "the ever-living Christ in His Body which is the Church." How very different this sounded from the words of a well-known Evangelical Church leader, who said to me, "Church? There is neither an Evangelical nor a Catholic Church. A Church of one sort or another occurs whenever two or three ordinary Christians pray together and Christ is thus Lord over them." As I had found out, there is truly a Church which depends on the reality of Christ. It is the Body that has absolute truth which it dispenses in its office of teacher of mankind and against which the "gates of hell shall not prevail." This Church is the mother that one can trust and in whose bosom man can find his sure refuge.

The Church is like a mother who tells her child things he does not yet understand. One must simply be able to wait with reverence as God's mother herself once had to, when her twelve-year-old Son spoke in the temple with such profound and authoritative words. The Holy Spirit will tell each one of us what he has to know at the appropriate time. Yes, humble reverence and silent listening is often more important than much noisy controversy; our *Dachmutter* had already taught us that. Later, some time after my ordination, I learned to understand Catholic moral theology. For a Protestant this is not easy until he realizes that one is here concerned with objective values such as truth and goodness, which are in conformity with God's law which is, as it were, part and parcel of His nature and which leads man and all the universe into His order. The Protestant has first to realize that virtue is not a cramped and presumptuous attitude but a genuine and mature living dependence upon God's grace which is inspired by total loyalty.

Thus in the faith I found certitude, peace, and something of the nature of true humility.

After a year of quiet study and prayer, at the end of 1949, I felt certain I should be able to become a Catholic. I then went to see the Church President Niemöller, who received my declaration in quite a friendly manner. After all, when he was living with several priests in the concentration camp he had seriously considered becoming a Catholic himself. It pains me greatly that this fellow fighter in the Confessing Church who was a competent man of God, shortly afterward, when engaged in political strife, represented me as the tool or victim of Catholic power politics.

At the beginning of 1950, I had a dangerous illness which lasted for three months and seemed to cast doubt upon everything. It was aggravated by some ugly arguments with the administration of my Church who dealt only with the material questions (termination of pension) and were unconcerned with my spiritual welfare.

But God was with me all this time and He suddenly caused me to be cured permanently, apparently by the medicine considered of little therapeutic value, which a new doctor gave me. Three days later, in April, 1950, I was discharged and I made the journey to Mainz, where Father zu Löwenstein received me into the Church in the chapel of the

Blessed Sacrament in the cathedral, and the bishop gave me my first Holy Communion in the chapel of the Heilig Grab monastery.

I felt as if I had walked into the void, for at that time I simply did not know how and where I was going to find a living. But such an act of faith is necessary for Evangelical clergymen as well; the larger the family, the greater is the act of faith.

After I had done this, the bishop of Mainz took an affectionate interest in me and my wife, and, in exchange for a little cooperation in the diocesan court, assured our livelihood. With his permission, I continued my studies, trusting in God's providence, for another year and a half at the seminary of Mainz. I commuted daily to Mainz and attended lectures there on pastoral theology, in addition to which I had tutors for dogmatic theology and the moral theology of the sacraments.

I was permitted twice, at the beginning and end of my study, to share the life of the seminary for a month, where the superior, Father Reuss, the present auxiliary bishop, helped me greatly with his most friendly aid and advice. The seminarians showed nothing but affection and understanding for their married fellow student who beat all age records, and they were also his constant and willing instructors in the liturgy.

Our bishop went to Rome in the autumn of 1950 to ask the Holy Father if my ordination would be approved under certain circumstances, and the permission arrived in April, 1951. (The Archbishop of Paderborn had already for some time concerned himself in this matter with Professor Höfer, his assistant, as the intermediary.) After passing orals in dogmatic theology and moral theology, I received holy orders from our bishop in the seminary church at Mainz on December 22, 1951. The next day, December 23, which was my seventy-first birthday, I was permitted to offer, with the guidance of our bishop, my first Mass in the chapel of the English Ladies (Institute of Mary) in Mainz. These excellent ladies instructed at their house many candidates from our circle for first Communion and confirmation.

Uncommon prominence was given to my first Mass by the presence of certain dignitaries. Among those who attended were Professor Höfer, sent by the archbishop of Paderborn; the gentlemen of the League of St. Willibrord in Holland; Professor Willebrands, the present secretary of the Catholic Ecumenical Conference; and Dr. Thyssen. Indeed, even the famous eighty-four-year-old anthropologist, Father Schmidt of Fribourg in Switzerland insisted on coming in spite of the winter cold. He was, in fact, connected with this ordination in a special way, for he was the first to suggest to the Holy Father the possibility of the ordination of the Evangelical pastors. We were already acquainted with him and had met him several times. He was so interested in our circle and especially in our *Dachmutter* that he dedicated an erudite study in one of his volumes to her. His fellow religious and friend, the former superior-general of the Society of the Divine Word, Father Grendel, was to our great regret, unable to be present at this ordination. This priest was the very soul of all the efforts that had been made to obtain this privilege. He was a true man of God, and he worked for our cause right up to his death.

In his sermon at my first Mass, Bishop Stohr spoke of the event in these terms: "The Holy Father's decision is to be understood in the light of his love for the Church, which tells our brethren that when they come over to us they will not be treated as second-class Christians, or as Christians with inferior rights, but they will share in everything. What would a mother not do to bring her children back. . . ."

On the first day of the Christmas festivities the bishop brought out in his sermon the meaning of my ordination. "We may hope, and we will pray longingly for it, that because of the happenings of these two days, we can call upon God with redoubled zeal to cause His grace to break through, so that finally we all may kneel together, united in heart and belief."

When I stood for the first time at the altar I realized that something wonderful was really happening, and I realize it afresh every time I am permitted to lend my voice and my hands to Christ at His holy altar. I also know it whenever I am permitted to give expression, by God's authority, to His mercy in the confessional with the *Ego te absolvo*. It is thus, through the Church, that my longing for wholeness, the certitude of solid tradition, and the reality of being have been fulfilled.

One other thing I recall about this first Mass was that I was conscious of the blessed nearness of our *Dachmutter*, who was rejoicing in her first priest.

A great storm arose in the press throughout almost the whole world on account of this ordination. Quite truthfully, we were uninterested in causing a sensation. But it is possible that God desired to make known to the hearts of many men what was happening here. I received 278 letters from bishops, priests, members of religious orders, and layfolks (Protestants, too), both at home and abroad. Almost all the letters (261) expressed approval or sent friendly greetings.

Some people have been anxious about the maintenance of priestly celibacy in general, but it should be noted our ordination does not in any way affect it. (A few others have followed who are also married, i.e., a young member of our circle, Otto Melchers, and another pastor; further ordinations are to come.) The privilege granted us applies only to an existing marriage. I myself who lived unmarried up to the age of forty-seven, can only say that I have the profoundest respect for the great sacrifice made by young priests in denying themselves a life companion. I acknowledge the eschatological significance of celibacy.

By our ordination we are permitted to dispense all the sacraments, but, out of respect for the existing norms in the parishes, we are to be chiefly engaged in less direct spiritual ministrations.

Since many distorted accounts appeared in the press, I found it necessary to write my "final word" which was published in many periodicals both inside Germany and abroad. At that time I also wrote a few words for the Belgians on the subject in connection with the Church Unity Octave. I replied in *Hochland* to an article by the Evangelical pastor of Offenbach, Lehmann, who addressed three questions to me in the *Lutherische Kirchenzeitung*.

Apart from this, most of my former Evangelical friends

remained silent. The Evangelical press service endeavored to play the event down, and the *Evangelischer Bund* tried to minimize it by a counterdemonstration.

I have been asked how a married priest uses his time. Believe me, there is plenty of work. At first I continued to live in Wiesbaden and assisted eagerly in Holy Trinity parish. I celebrated Mass, preached, heard confessions, and concerned myself with all sorts of official business. Together with my wife I undertook the instruction of converts, and the parish expressed its complete confidence in us. Representing the bishop of Mainz, I conducted negotiations with the Ministry of Religion. People with inquiries about Catholicism, and people who are just seeking, come to me almost daily. At the request of the bishop, I have spoken at almost all of the conferences of the diocese of Mainz. Moreover, I have also given many lectures in the surrounding dioceses on the development of the Evangelical Church from the time of Luther to the Ecumenical Movement and also on my own experiences. I have also been permitted to visit many parishes, professional people, and teachers, and I have been amazed over and over again at the enthusiasm shown by priests and laymen for the idea of Christian reunion.

In April, 1953, my wife and I, after an introduction by our bishop, were received in an unforgettable private audience by the Holy Father in Rome. It was his first audience after his almost fatal illness of that year. I was very grateful to be able to thank him personally for the great kindness with which he had opened the door to the priesthood to me and my brethren. He received my wife very graciously. The impression his personality made was quite extraordinary.

The light of eternity seemed to shine through the nature of this tall ascetic figure and through all his words, as the sun shines through a vessel of pure crystal. That which we immediately thought of at the tomb of St. Peter, below the great dome of the papal basilica, became to us a living certainty, that is that the See of Peter stands fast against all the powers of the world and the devil.

The Holy Father's blessing strengthened me in my new office as priest. I was able during these days in Rome to offer the Holy Sacrifice at the tomb of the Prince of Apostles, deep under the earth, facing the figure of St. Pius X in his glass coffin below the altar. I also said Mass close to the tomb of St. Vincent Pallotti and at the altar in the church of St. Mary Major at which Pope Pius XII said his first Mass. In this church one becomes especially conscious of all the abounding love of God's holy Mother. Later I had the great pleasure of speaking of my pilgrimage to the young students of the *Germanicum* and of kindling their enthusiasm for the reunion of Christendom.

In Assisi, among the hills of Umbria, we felt the presence of that magnificent reformer of the Middle Ages, St. Francis, who, by his "littleness," his meekness, and his simple obedience became incomparably greater than the man who stands so high in his own estimation at the threshold of "modern times." At his grave I was able to feel small with him before the great and merciful God.

Former members of my parish, who had been converted in the meantime, or who had this step in mind, crossed our path in Rome by some strange "coincidence."

A Pallottine Father from Limburg had been an extremely

friendly guide during these days in Rome. When, later on, I remarked on his great kindness, he wrote telling me he had been imprisoned by the Gestapo for seventeen months in Frankfort, and that for seven of these months he had had neither occupation nor books. For this reason he had done much praying, and, in obedience to an inner inspiration, he had also prayed for the reunion of the separated brethren in the province of Nassau-Hesse. He had prayed that the Holy Ghost would inspire the pope to allow married Evangelical pastors to receive ordination with this aim for unification in view. He said to me, "When you came I saw my prayer fulfilled."

Our bishop, with his farsighted ecumenical views, had a house built in Mainz which is now an information center for matters of belief. It is here that a second married priest, Otto Melchers, lives with his family, together with my wife and myself. We have undertaken the counseling and instruction of all those seeking the Faith, and we give further assistance to converts and ecumenical instruction to priests and the laity. The name of the house, *Domus pacis,* indicates clearly that its purpose is not that of a center of propaganda or warfare against those of other faiths, but that of a refuge of peace which exists to give expression to God's peace in the establishment of peace among Christians.

In order to prepare ourselves thoroughly for this work I went with my wife to Holland for some weeks. There, as guests of the Dutch League of St. Willibrord, we were able to study the activities of many centers which exist to spread the faith, such as the *Una Sancta,* the *Open deur* (Open Door), and the houses and homes of the Ladies of Bethany.

It became immediately apparent that everyone works for these centers as members of the lay apostolate, without selfish concern. All their effort is made entirely in unity with the Holy Spirit. What sacrifices they make there for oneness in the faith! In many a lecture, all the way up to Friesland, I was able to speak to open hearts of my life pilgrimage and of the ecclesiastical developments in Germany.

And in Cologne, on our way back, we were greeted by the Dominican provincial of Germany who was active everywhere, giving lectures and sermons in the service of *Una Sancta*. In this city we also found that a center similar to ours has already been begun.

We discovered enthusiasm everywhere for the cause of the one Shepherd and the one flock.

Now that I have completed my narrative, I wonder if it has made clear that God still performs miracles, as He always has, that He is doing something in our day to let us know that He desires the unity of Christianity, and that He desires it *today*. The door which Pius XII opened to the Evangelical clergy, respecting as he did their office, their marriages, and their desire for unity, has in reality been opened by God Himself as a sort of divine enticement toward the fullness of His mercy and love. Hence, we have no doubts now as to what His intentions are. Anyone who has had his eyes opened to God's activity, will see this intention everywhere in the world today.

It is no accident that God has brought together Catholics and Protestants in the armed forces, in graves, in prisons, and in concentration camps, and that He has dispersed them from their homes to dwell among those who live according to a different faith. Moreover, it is not just by chance that He has brought the confessions together in common political activity and that He gave the Protestants their new theological outlook, the new endeavor for Church unity and sacramental integrity manifested in their vast world congresses; and that at the same time He gave the Catholic the biblical and liturgical movement, so that by these means both sides were drawn considerably closer together.

And again, why do we hear a loud clamor for Church unity from the mission field, from the young churches in the backward areas of the world that are engaged in a daily struggle with paganism and bolshevism? And why have so many fences disappeared behind which various groups of Christians used to sit entrenched too securely?

Almost no one would have believed this situation possible at the beginning of the century, when I first began to study. Today those who are perceptive, aware of the undercurrents of history, know that the rivers of God are flowing unseen in the depths like the glacier stream under ice. A lady who is a teacher and a Catholic wrote to me on the occasion of my first Mass. It seems that in her childhood in Offenbach her mother once heard that I had prayed from the chancel of the town church for the newly-elected Pope Pius XII, and had requested the congregation to pray for him at this time in the Catholic churches which were always open. The mother told her children, "From now on, we will say the Rosary daily for that parson," and they continued this for several years. Of course, I had not the vaguest idea that I was being supported by these prayers. And, it was through such revelations as these that I became more aware of the hidden work of God, realizing that He gives us His graces in our times just as He always had in the past.

It was in Germany that the religious breach started long ago, and it is in Germany that the reunification of Christians must begin again.

It was from the see of Mainz that the division originated, and today it is from the see of Mainz that the cry for reconciliation goes forth.

It is perhaps one of the supreme sacred ironies of our times that the path Luther trod leads right back into the innermost heart of the Catholic Church.

The door is open.

MARTIN GIEBNER | *From Distress to Fulfillment*

THE CONTENT OF MY NARRATIVE has been determined by the trend of this book. I intend to describe here the paths by which I was led to my conversion.

The conjunction of my personal experiences with theoretical considerations will considerably banish the danger of my giving the reader a bit of dry reading. I have made up my mind about two things. One of these is that no word in my account shall give any material to sensation-mongers, the other is that I intend to adhere faithfully to my principle of objective truth, of writing nothing with a view to pleasing or hurting anyone. I do not want my Protestant brethren who read these lines to be offended. I beg them, too, not to condemn me for leaving their ranks, and this applies in particular to my High-Church friends.

Finally, I beg all my readers, of whatever communion, to try to understand this contribution on the basis of its true spirit, that reality to which all the rest is attuned and which consists of a grateful joy in having reached the goal which God in His mercy has prescribed.

First contacts with the Catholic Church

The longer I live and the more I arrange the events of my life in the order of their development, the more significant does the day of my baptism appear. I received the sacrament in the lofty cathedral of St. Peter in Bautzen. This cathedral is the seat of the bishop of Meissen, and it is shared by both faiths. Two-thirds of the cathedral is reserved for Protestant worship; the other third (the choir), for Catholic worship. A lattice screen divides this Gothic church into the two areas of worship; a significant piece of the church history of Upper Saxony, irrevocable since 1635, is documented thereby. The cathedral dean, Leisentritt, a loyal son of his Church, boldly championed the Catholic cause during the confusion of the Reformation period, and he managed to preserve at least a part of the cathedral for the use of Catholics.

Not very far from the high altar of the Catholic part of the cathedral stands the baptismal font of the Protestant parish. It is there that our Lord first took hold of my soul and impressed upon it the indelible sign of my belonging to Him. I do not wish to indulge in any speculation here as to whether the proximity of the Eucharistic Saviour, indicated by the burning light in the Catholic part of the cathedral, had any influence upon me as a child. Such speculations are abortive, for God alone knows the answer.

But I do know for a fact that God's providence bound me to this cathedral again and again. I was confirmed in it. Later on, I became a member of the cathedral choir when I was one of the grammar school boys, who, following an ancient tradition, performed the service there on Sundays. From our choir loft there, which was directly opposite the altar of the Catholic part of the cathedral I sometimes watched the celebration of High and Low Mass. And this was at a time when I was just deciding upon the study of theology. Shortly before leaving for the Front in 1914, when I was a candidate for the ministry, I preached a sermon in the cathedral. And even today, this dual church appears to me to be deeply significant.

The grating there is a symbol of an anti-Christian and, hence, impossible situation. It is an emphatic warning to us to keep in our minds the Saviour's words, "That they may all be one," and to use all our strength to bring about the fruition of this desire.

The grammar school of my native town, conducted on "humanistic" principles, was open to students of both faiths. For religious instruction we were separated. But all the students gathered together in the assembly hall for Monday devotions, participating in choral singing and prayers, and, every day of the week, devotions were carried out in a similar manner in the classrooms. I think our Catholic students received a good deal of stimulation from this, but we Protestant schoolboys made no comparable contact with Catholic life. In the upper grades the history of the Reformation was studied and it was taught from a distinctly Protestant point of view. At that time there was no *Una Sancta* movement, and Professor Lortz had not yet written his epoch-making work on the Reformation in Germany. Thus, we students obtained a false picture of the conditions in the medieval Catholic Church, which, unfortunately, one simply projected as still existing at the present time. The impression that could not be avoided was that it was a good thing that Luther had come along and cleaned up the mess. The fact, however, that God permitted the Reformation, but that the Catholic Church continued in spite of it, since it was firmly grounded upon the rock of Peter, did not occur to us.

Religious development in student days—1911-1914

My theological studies began at Tübingen, I entered the seminary with the pure faith of a child. The years of adolescence, it is true, had known some doubts about the existence of God, but I never missed saying my prayers, nor did I fail to go to church occasionally in the years following my confirmation. We were taken to the sacrament of the Lord's Supper twice during the school year. But in the seminary, there was a professor whose reflections upon the Gospel of St. Mark were based on considerations of philology and religious history. I became familiar with the fundamental principle of Protestantism, i.e., the completely unhindered, subjective interpretation of Holy Scripture, controlled by no teaching office and bound to no tradition. A number of views were put forward. Which was one to accept? The lecturer did not express his own opinion about the decisive parts, but left the student to decide for himself. He frequently concluded his lectures with such words as, "We are left with a *non liquet*," or "All we can say is *nescimus*." Quite unintentionally, of course, this had the psychological effect of dealing a shattering blow to the authority of Holy Scripture, and incidentally to that of the professor, also. The Gospel of St. Mark had descended to the position of a mere literary product of ancient times, which was not seen in the frame of the background of the Church but explained in a purely scientific manner. I fear that this gentleman, well meaning as he might have been, had no living connection with the Church. He was a learned man, a professor, but he was not a priest obliged at times to enter the pulpit or approach the altar of God.

An example from one of my later parishes will reveal to what extent this method of interpreting the Bible, or having it interpreted, has unconsciously obtained a hold upon the minds of many "educated" Protestants. A jurist, an official connected with an industrial concern, once explained to me in conversation why he never went to church. "I am a humanist," he said, "I can read my New Testament at home." I was firmly convinced that he had no New Testament at all, and, even if he had, never read it. But he was of the opinion that preaching was identical with a sort of academic lecturing which was offered to those who were unfamiliar with Greek. One sees just how poor was this typical, modern intellectual's view of the value of a Protestant service.

During my period at Tübingen, a lawsuit was brought against Pastor Carl Jatho of Cologne, whose liberal sermons had offended the church authorities. A former Swabian pastor, named Schrempf, made use of this opportunity to call a meeting of the students of all the faculties in Tübingen and to invite the professors of Protestant theology to debate the pros and cons of the cases of Jatho and Schrempf. It seems that the argument turned chiefly upon the Apostles' Creed with special vehemence against the Virgin Birth, the Resurrection of the Lord, and the immortality of the soul. Schrempf had been obdurate. He was solidly on Jatho's side. He had declared his opinions before the consistory and admitted the heresy. He had thereupon been deprived of his office.

The Tübingen assembly was not exactly peaceful. The professors, whose leader was old Adolf Schlatter, a Swiss, were not altogether effective in their own defense, if I remember rightly. As can be imagined, the result of such experiences was that many a young Protestant theologian became a sceptic.

At that time the fact that no one really undertook to concern himself with us young theologians was a fault which was particularly striking. The so-called "open" evenings in the company of some Tübingen professors were chiefly devoted to sociability, and there was little opportunity for private discussion or spiritual guidance.

The Catholic seminarian was better off. He had the connection with his Church and with the sacraments. He had teachers who were priests and who were under the jurisdiction of their bishop. This fact is of great significance, because it guarantees the existence of a clergy which is by no means ignorant, but which is thoroughly educated in the *faith*. We Protestant theologians heard nothing but "pulpit lectures" from our professors in our divine service at the seminary, though these addresses were, of course, in a framework of prayer. But none of our teachers ever approached the altar. In the collegiate church of Tübingen the altar stood on one side as a silent memorial of ancient times, its only function being that of a museum-piece.

That, then, was Tübingen in the year 1911, the Tübingen that had once had the bold idea of conferring with the Eastern Church with the object of finding a basis for union with her. But that was long ago.

In spite of the college of my childhood faith, I was audacious enough to continue my theological studies in the University of Leipzig. With gratitude I acknowledge my deep indebtedness to the influence of the dogmatic theologian, Ludwig Ihmels, who later became the first provincial bishop of Saxony. His lectures and, particularly, his sermons, which he prepared conscientiously and which he was still committing to memory in the sacristy while the congregation were singing the sermon hymn, witnessed to the fact that this man was earnest and vitally interested in his religion.

On the other hand, the lectures of the professor of moral theology made the exclusiveness of Protestantism very apparent. When this professor announced that, as president of the Gustav-Adolph-Verein,[1] he had consecrated the Protestant church in Rome and had, on this occasion, also visited St. Peter's and attended a service there, the impression his description made upon me was painful. For him the two most important things were the overwhelming munificence of this, the largest church in the world, and then, the fact that he and his companion had openly borne witness to their different faith by standing during the Consecration when the faithful had fallen to their knees. The majority of Protestants, of course, do not believe in the substantial change. This same gentleman—he was also the other university-preacher—once criticized his colleague, Professor Ihmels, in a characteristic manner. In a lecture dealing with liturgical deportment, he expressed the view that a clergyman who had assisted in the distribution of the Lord's Supper should join the congregation as soon as he had completed his service, and not, as Ihmels had once done, await the conclusion of the sacred action while standing before the altar to receive the blessing before going with his fellow clergymen into the sacristy. That would smack too much of the acolyte! These and other trifling experiences took a firm hold upon my memory, because they resembled small bits of stone with

1 The Gustav-Adolf-Verein is a society to aid Protestant Churches in non-Protestant areas.

which a mosaic could be pieced together, a mosaic that revealed to me the inward disunity of the Protestant Church, which, nevertheless, like the Dying Gladiator, is ready to strike a blow at some fancied opponent—which is usually some aspect of Catholicism.

The lectures delivered in Leipzig on the New and Old Testament were very like those of Tübingen. The Holy Scripture became the object of philological research. The treatment of the various Lutheran creeds or those of the Church as a whole, given by a certain liberal lecturer, lacked just one thing: reverence for God's revelations. There was a word that I never heard, which Catholic theology employs when confronted with a dogma, and that word is *mystery*. This word was not in the vocabulary of that dogmatic theologian. Later on, in the year 1930, when the jubilee of the Augsburg Confession was being celebrated, this same gentleman declared openly that the New Protestantism would be anathema to the Augsburg confessors. "We would not be regarded by them as the sons of Augsburg," he writes, and adds with shattering clarity, "Let us make no mistake about our apostasy from 1530!" And, yet, for many, the New Protestantism was really the logical continuation of the Reformation. "We must not stop where Luther stopped," they say, "but grasp the mentality of the great Reformer" and "in Luther's stride go further than Luther"! [2] This New Protestantism would not then be apostasy, but a further development on the original Lutheran lines.

With such experiences to "arm" them, the young theologians prepared themselves for office. (The consequences be-

[2] Heiler, *Im Ringen um die Kirche*, p. 448.

came clear when the German Christians came into being under Hitler.) Indeed, even during their course of study, some fellow students declared that it was impossible for them to become pastors. They would prefer to become schoolteachers, they said. Later, we learned what these "liberal-thinkers" gave to their students in the training colleges when, in 1918, after the dissolution of the German Empire, these teachers came forward as speakers in the assemblies of those who had left the Church. We heard there an echo from the colleges of the lords of the New Protestantism, but now it was in the form of hostile opposition from the mouths of half-educated people.

University studies came to an abrupt end with the outbreak of World War I. The emergency examination was followed by military service at home and on the Front until December, 1916. Because I had become disabled, I was exempted from further service. During a furlough, I had taken my second examination, and so I went as an inexperienced curate to Bad Schandau in Saxon Switzerland. In normal times how glad I would have been to continue my studies; but this was not to be, as I shall relate later.

Ordination, assignment, experiences in the ministry

On my ordination on December 3, 1916, I heard the oath by which I was to be bound. I trust my readers will be indulgent if I deviate from my narrative a bit to explain a few salient points about this and other documents. It stressed that I was "to teach and preach, pure and undefiled, to the best of my knowledge and judgment, the gospel of Christ as it is contained in Holy Scripture and in the first unaltered Augsburg Confession and declared later in other creedal documents of the Evangelical Lutheran Church." This obligation was laid upon my soul later at each change of office.

The patent of ordination, worded completely in Old Church style, has become for me a really important document. I have often re-read it. Written in Latin, it begins with the glorious words, "Non alia vox in coelo et in terra unquam ardentior audita est quam precatio Filii Dei in agone, in qua petit colligi et servari Ecclesiam et sic regi, ut unum sit in Deo" ("Never has another voice in heaven or on earth been heard with more urgency than the prayer of the Son of God in His agony, in which He prays that the Church may be so gathered, preserved, and guided that it may be one in God").

The document closes with the words of 1 Timothy 4:13, "Attende lectioni, adhortationi et doctrinae. Ne negligas donum, quod datum est tibi per prophetiam cum impositione manuum coetus seniorum" ("Be diligent in reading, exhortation and doctrine. Do not neglect the gift, which was given to thee through prophecy with the imposition of the hands of the assemblage of the elders"). [The Greek has *presbyteroi;*—the Vulgate renders this as *presbyterii;* the Douai Version translates as "priesthood" rather than the "assemblage of elders."] By these words it is admitted that great significance is to be ascribed to ordination. Even today the Protestant Church, especially the Evangelical Lutheran Church, lays great stress on the value of ordination, but it is anxious to avoid giving the impression that a sacrament is involved. And yet everything is so simple when one carefully considers the apostle's words and draws conclusions: the imposition of the hands, the assemblage of the elders. Whence do the assemblage of the elders have the authority to impose their hands? By reason of apostolic succession, by intending to do what the Church does; yes, and at the end of the chain stands the Lord Himself. But the Protestants do not wish to go so far, for it would put them in a difficult position: they would be forced to recognize ordination as a sacrament. After all, they do not wish to go that far in the direction of Catholic doctrine.

Many years later, I had to appeal to this patent of ordination before my superiors, some of whom, it is probable, had no such document. In fact, documents in this form have not been issued for a long time now. There is now a completely new form which has been provided by the Liturgical Commission of the Evangelical Lutheran Churches [3] that still has the words of St. Paul to Timothy concerning reading and the rest which are repeated when the Bible is handed over, immediately after the "conveyance" of the office of the Church, as a sign that the newly-ordained minister has now taken over the service of the Word and the Sacrament. However, this patent deliberately omits the injunction concerning the gift that is granted through the imposition of hands. (I would like to affirm that I have not been unfaithful to my ordination oath, but I have understood it better as the years have passed.) At first I had sincere doubts as to the meaning

[3] Composed by the liturgical commission of the United Evangelical Lutheran Church of Germany and published by the hierarchy of this Church in 1952.

of the words in the oath: "the unaltered Augsburg Confession," for there is an altered one which owes its origin to Melancthon. Moreover, I did not know just what to think of the words, "other creedal writings of the Evangelical Lutheran Church," because among these are Luther's Schmalkaldic Articles with their savage polemics against the Catholic Church. How can all this fit together? The Augsburg Confession is a pacific document, whereas the Schmalkaldic Articles sound the clarion of war. What the Augsburg Confession affirms, the Articles deny, for in them Luther goes so far as to denounce the pope as the antichrist, and in one passage refuses any possibility of reconciliation with the Catholic Church: "Sic scilicet in aeternum disjungimur et contrarii invicem sumus" ("Thus we are and shall remain forever separate and opposed to one another"). The patent of ordination, however, speaks of the Lord's solicitude that the Church may be so led *"ut unum sit in Deo."* Of course. But Luther did not see the Catholic Church as *the* Church. Was then the Protestant Church the Church? It was with such questions in my mind that I began the long and difficult struggle.

And now to resume my narrative. I found I was quite busy in my position as curate, especially since it was Advent and the charge of Bad Schandau consisted of five village parishes. Moreover, I was quite alone there, for the vicar was ill in bed.

I should like to mention a few of my recollections of this period. It was with astonishment that I saw the way in which the clergy carried out their ministry when, from time to

time, they came to Bad Schandau to help. Their views about
the sacraments varied greatly, and they treated the liturgy
quite arbitrarily. The congregations at celebrations of the
Lord's Supper were very small, and there were few opportunities given to receive the sacrament in the first place.
The rite was a hole-and-corner affair, considered merely an
unimportant appendix to the service and denied almost any
prominence. It was a fact that I myself knew very little of
the ceremonies, even the administration of baptism. It
sounds incredible, but this training was not included in my
course of preparation for the office. In my years at the university scarcely any practical instruction had been given.
Dealing with such practical activities might have seemed too
little the business of academic training. And the ritual offered very little help in regard to basic liturgical practice.
I did know just a little about the liturgy of the Lord's Supper, because, when I was a schoolboy and in the choir at the
cathedral, I had seen the clergy of my native town minis-
tering at the altar. But my penetration into the nature of
the sacraments was not sufficiently deep. I was a Lutheran
curate and at the same time not one.

The first Christmas in my new post was a bitter disap-
pointment for me. Christmas Eve passed without a divine
service, and on Christmas Day everything was just as usual,
the same black gown, the same monotonous liturgy (in spite
of the fact that a festal form was available) and no celebration of the sacred banquet. It was just a Sunday like any
other Sunday. The only thing which in any way indicated
the significance of the day was the Christmas tree beside the

altar. I began to think of a remedy for all this. I resolved
that the next Christmas would be different, if my vicar had
nothing against it.

At the church conferences, the older clergy were occupied with the problem of confirmation, the interpretation of
which was so relative that confusion prevailed. This caused
some trouble, although church life generally pursued its
course along good, though possibly rather uneven, roads.
This situation, tenuous though it was, existed because we
still had the monarchy, and because the education system
was officially on our side. Yet there was a certain vague atmosphere of uncertainty, and things were just the same when
I left the ministry after thirty-four years of service. This condition seems to be endemic and it is difficult to see how it
can be eliminated. Many of my former colleagues go to the
annual confirmation celebrations with very mixed feelings.

The High Church Union

The Reformation Jubilee of 1917 was the prelude to
many celebrations in honor of Martin Luther which lasted
until 1946. Almost all the events of the Reformation period
and Luther's personal life were duly commemorated. There
was no lack of celebrations. Frequently, I could not shake off
the feeling that these celebrations were being used as a sort
of secret elixir, a tonic for the Protestantism of those people
whose faith was well in decline. Moreover, it was confidently
expected that this propaganda would be more effectual if it
were offered as an allopathic medicine against Rome, the
Catholic Church, etc.

But there was one event, historically significant, which was passed over in silence. That was the discussion Luther had with Zwingli in Marburg in 1529. As a result of this Luther saved the sacrament of the altar for the Protestant Evangelical Church.

It is deserving of special emphasis that, among the large amount of literature published for the Reformation Jubilee, one particular book was presented to the Protestant Church, then rejoicing over its birthday in 1517, which differed violently from all the other publications. Although the others glorified the achievement of Wittenberg in many high-sounding phrases, this book struck a note of penitence and was entitled *VC Stimuli et clavi* ("95 Goads and Nails": cf. Eccles. 12:11). The author was H. Hansen, a Lutheran clergyman in a northern German parish.

In splendid Latin, Hansen, a clergyman grown old in the ministry, reminds his own Evangelical Church, and indeed all Christians, of the first words that Luther put forth in his "95 Theses," "When our Lord Christ says, 'Do Penance,' He wishes our whole life to be a life of penance. . . ." Hansen enlarges upon this idea and calls upon the Protestant Church in unmistakable terms when he says, "Protestantism [in the Latin text it is even *Protestantismus qui dicitur*] has no reason to celebrate jubilees but good reasons to do penance in sackcloth and ashes!"

These words found an echo in the hearts of many, including the laity. They started a movement which culminated in the foundation in Berlin of the High Church Union on October 9, 1918, a month before the collapse of the German Empire. The object of this Union was to bring aid to the Protestant Churches which, as everyone could see, were having difficulties. I did not see the first notice of this novel Union, but I became acquainted with the movement only later when I saw a report in a secular newspaper of some of their activities. I communicated with the executive of the movement and received in reply a copy of the principles of the movement which had been approved in 1918. I should like to mention here a few of these ideas as follows:

1. The High Church Union aims at reorganizing the churches of the Reformation in regard to their constitution and worship. With this object in view, it seeks the complete independence of these churches [plural] in ecclesiastical affairs and church government.

2. The Church [here singular] is the visible institution founded by Christ and the apostles for the salvation of mankind. She must, for this reason, be allowed an influence upon the national life which is appropriate to her great importance. In Protestant Christianity the consciousness of belonging to the universal Church of Christ must be awakened.

3. With these objects in view, the High Church Union thinks that an episcopal constitution, such as is thoroughly conformable with the spirit of Holy Scripture, is needed.

Here, for the first time in the history of the Reformation churches, there was a demand for a genuinely episcopal constitution. To make this demand, real courage was needed. The *summus episcopus* of the Protestant Church of Prussia was Wilhelm II, king of Prussia and German emperor, who was a layman from an ecclesiastical point of view. With him, the other Protestant sovereigns functioned as the bishops of their territories. In the kingdom of Saxony the Catholic king was in fact the bishop of the Evangelical Lutheran State Church, but he allowed himself to be represented by the state ministers commissioned *in evangelicis.* The High Church Union set its face against this grotesque system, and this was an affront to the authority of the state. What the Union was asking for looked like revolution because it refused the princes a statutory right. To begin with, and this was before the collapse of the imperial power, the Union pointed to the state of neglect to which the Protestant Church had fallen. Then it pointed out that from the beginning, the Church had placed its government wholly in the hands of secular princes and their state machinery. Luther, who, when he considered giving the incipient Protestant Church a head, had said that this could wait, was no organizer, and his shortsightedness bore bitter fruit. He could not foresee the needs of the future. The Union had the merit of having directed attention to Luther's omission just in time, at the last hour.

And finally, two further proposals of the High Church Union that I would like to record are:

4. It wished preaching to occupy a much less prominent place, and this was to be done by pointing up and emphasizing the significance and objective character of the sacraments. Soon afterward, it was demanding the recognition of seven sacraments, claiming that in order to maintain the integrity of these sacraments, the fact that they must be dispensed in accordance with ecclesiastical ordinances was an

essential prerequisite. As a result, richer liturgical rites for divine services, additional altar ornaments, and more colorful vestments were advocated.

5. It was suggested that the practice of confession and the Lord's Supper be reformed. Private confession, pious exercises, Protestant conventual life, and the use of the breviary for clerics were recommended.

If after thirty-six years, one reads all these proposals, which were still far from being clearly expressed, and compares them with the present situation in the Protestant Church, it is amazing to note the extent to which these suggestions have been carried out by many Evangelical Churches. To some extent they have accepted the title of bishop for their leaders, they seek the reintroduction of a "German Mass," and they would like to resume private confessions as the crown of their spiritual revivals.

As for the expansion of the liturgy, mentioned above, it is interesting to observe that one can confirm with genuine pleasure that the proposed ritual for the Evangelical Lutheran churches and parishes provides a complete Ordinary and Proper for the main service, complete with sacristy preparation. The Introit is used and the Confiteor is recited by the celebrant and the other ministers, such as the lector, cantor, organist, sacristan, churchwardens, and choir-singers. Hence, one can state with confidence that there is a "German Mass," analogous to that which Luther recommended in 1526. The action of the minister giving himself communion is included for the first time. What progress! The words repeated when the sacrament is dispensed are in order, "May the Body of our Lord Jesus Christ preserve thee unto life everlasting." Unfortunately, the action stops short of the summit. It turns back, as it were, because the operation of the mystery in its completeness would not ring true. However praiseworthy it is that the communicant should say, "Lord, I am not worthy that Thou shouldst enter under my roof," it is evident that this humble confession only has actual meaning in regard to the objectivity of the Real Presence. The last step is not taken. One cannot, one dare not, take it, because of Luther. Bread remains bread. The whole post-Luther controversy opens up again. Although the celebrant says, "The Body of the Lord," the communicant understands in his heart, and adds, "in, with, and under the bread." The main thing is missing. No heart beats in this "Mass," because Luther excised it from the Catholic Mass, and there is no transubstantiation. A return to the Apostolic Succession is what is needed in the Evangelical Lutheran Churches. Among the clergy there is unfortunately, practically no understanding of the significance of this. Furthermore, the teaching office is missing; in this respect the Protestant churches have no unity of doctrine. Perhaps it can be seen in the declaration issued by the Lutheran bishops on the Catholic dogma of the Assumption in 1950 that some attempt at dogmatic decision is being made that could be applicable to the various provinces.

The Catholic tendency of these proposals of the High Church Union is unmistakable. And, however much Lutherans insist that they want to remain Protestant, and this Pastor Hansen did with emphasis, it is completely clear to me that today the Universal Church, and therefore the Lord Himself, is calling. A long process of regeneration has been initiated by the High Church Union, and everyone who experienced it desired nothing more than that it should come to a good end.

The proposals of the High Church Union received a great deal of publicity. Numerous applications for membership were registered by the clergy and laity alike. Leading personalities in the ecclesiastical world and members of the consistories and similar Church bodies remained silent, but they kept a watchful eye on the progress of events. I know of only one Church dignitary who openly spoke in defense of the Union. The professor of moral theology in Leipzig, whom I have already mentioned above, was the only one who came forward with a disparaging remark. He said that the High Church Union was an "association which wanted to reform the clothing regulations of the Protestant clergy." He was here criticizing the use of the chasuble in the celebration of the "German Mass." Yet he could not have been unaware of the fact that the chasuble was worn in the Protestant divine service right up to the middle of the eighteenth century, and that it was Friedrich Wilhelm I who in 1733 had first forbidden, by a royal cabinet order, the wearing of Mass vestments. As the *summus episcopus* he had his rights. But, unfortunately, our professor chose to see only the most obviously obtrusive externals.

I was personally attracted by the richer liturgical significance of the services and the sacraments. Unfortunately, I had no knowledge of the first great rally of the High Church Union in Saxony. This was held in Chemnitz, and after seeing a report of this assembly, I joined the Union in 1921.

At this time the Union had gone one step further in the accentuation of some very important points. This fact was quite clearly expressed in the form of application for membership. The applicant affirmed with his signature his belief in the three creeds of the Church (the Nicene, the Apostles', and the Athanasian), as well as in the Augsburg Confession in which, in any case, these creeds were contained. Thus the High Church Union was very obviously a dogmatic movement.

This revival brought to light a fearful and destructive ulcer in the very marrow of Protestantism. There were indeed plenty of clergy, like Jatho and Schrempf, whom we have already mentioned, who no longer believed in many important revelations of God: the Virgin Birth, the Resurrection or the immortality of the soul. However, the High Church Union built a dam against this faithlessness, because its rules were based upon, and derived only from, the faith itself. It was this foundation of faith which made the Union an effective protagonist for the objective validity of the sacraments. The movement was truly Catholic in the broadest sense of the word.

After I had joined, it seemed that I was on the right track, the track from which I had been thrown in consequence of my university studies. Divine Providence was leading me by way of liturgical interests to the affirmation of the basic truths of the faith. I was on the way to the Church. For this reason, I thank, after God, the High Church Union for my "theological existence today," to borrow an expression from Karl Barth.

High-Church work resulting from membership in the High Church Union

After four years of activity as curate and deacon, I was appointed pastor of Bad Schandau. Matins and Vespers of the old liturgical type were introduced, and the official journal of the High Church Union, *Die Hochkirche,* made many useful suggestions along these lines. The Magnificat and the Benedictus, both of which were in the hymnal used in our Saxon province, but were never sung, as well as the Te Deum (in translation) were made accessible to the congregation. Further, I succeeded in obtaining and erecting a beautiful and valuable altar from Dresden which improved the atmosphere of the main church in town because the previous bareness had not been conducive to devotion or to an attitude of worship. I made many enemies by doing this, although later, when the work was successfully accomplished at the end of a singlehanded struggle, the result was acknowledged with enthusiasm.

It was my cherished intention to bring back to the town an altar of the Blessed Mother which had stood for hundreds of years in Bad Schandau in a tiny church which had just recently fallen into ruins. The altar had been sold by my predecessor to an antiquarian society of Dresden "because of its Catholic character and consequent lack of value to the church authorities." It was High-Church practice to honor the sublime Mother, our Blessed Lady, but I was unable to obtain the restored altar. It finally perished in the flames which destroyed the museum in the Grossen Garten when Dresden was gutted in 1945.

Instead, a more authentically valuable altar of sandstone, which had stood from 1570 to 1760 in the church of the Holy Cross and later, until 1906, in St. Anne's Church was brought into our church. It was completely restored and erected with the help of the consistory and the State of Saxony, which was keenly interested in the preservation of this work of art. The financial end of the matter was entirely up to me and I had to get the parishioners to help. It was fortunate that just at that time, 1927, the Zwinger [4] in Dresden was being restored, and we were able to make use in Bad Schandau of the experience gained in that work and of the workers who had been employed there. The significant middle section of the altarpiece is a scene that shows Christ at the Last Supper. By this portrayal the true character of the Church was significantly presented, indicating the sacrament of the altar, the source of all life.

I began to lead the parish more deeply into the life of faith and ventured upon lectures in the spirit of the High Church. I first dealt with the Apostles' Creed. My next intention was to lead the people back to the sanctuary, to the sacraments, making their life in the Church consist of something more than vocal prayer or listening to sermons. Thus there was an objective foundation to their faith which was based on the verities which the Church has proposed for belief from the very beginning.

Efforts to obtain valid orders

One year, on the feast of St. Bartholomew, I was invited

4 Begun in 1711, it was intended as a vestibule to the royal palace; it is now a museum and art gallery.

to preach at a High-Church service in Berlin. In the sacristy of St. George's church in the Alexanderplatz (this church no longer stands), I laid the rochet over my gown and the stole was handed to me, the question suddenly occurred to me, "Have you a right to wear it?" The stole is the symbol of the priestly office, but I was no priest because I was simply ordained for a national church. Even if the dean had followed the ritual, and used the words, "I ordain thee . . . ," this was still no genuine ordination, but a sort of "quasi-ordination." (Later on, I was to claim that the words "I ordain thee" were used, but this was denied by the highest authorities of the Lutheran Church.) At any rate, the ordainer certainly had no intention "of doing what the Church does," quite apart from the fact that he himself had not been validly ordained.

Now I was faced with the problem my desiring valid orders! I wanted my proper place in the spiritual hierarchy of the Church. If I did not have it, all my activities, all my efforts in the realm of theology *per se* and, consequently, in its practical application, were left hanging in the air. Some of my High-Church friends experienced the same dilemma. Thus at an important stage in the early development of High-Church principles, a further stimulus was provided to increase the demand for an episcopal constitution. An episcopal constitution was very desirable, but it would have little meaning without the basis of episcopal succession. The question was whether or not the official regional churches were prepared to put their new bishops into this succession which could be proved to come from apostolic times; they had been unprepared to do this up to now.

The first provincial bishop of Saxony, the Professor Ihmels already mentioned, could have been consecrated by the Swedish Archbishop, Nathan Söderblom, but he declined. Did the Holy Spirit prevent him? (Cf. Acts 16:6.) "It is not opportune, not advisable," were Ihmels' words. He felt that it was impossible because of his respect for his colleagues who would not understand his action and who would strenuously oppose it. Those who had already raised objections when the bells had been rung on the occasion of the visit of the provincial bishop to a local town would be even less inclined to accept a consecrated bishop. Consequently, the High Church Union had to recognize from the beginning that it could not count on finding any sympathy for its views in the regional churches. And it certainly would not obtain it, either, if it sought permission for its clergy to acquire valid orders privately, in order thus to be ranked in the apostolic succession.

I have received information, but only by verbal effort, of all the efforts to obtain valid orders. I know that people turned first to Sweden, but the doors were closed to them. The fact that Bishop Ihmels had once declined consecration at the hands of Archbishop Söderblom remained too vivid a memory, besides which, the Church of Sweden wanted to be sure at least of the consent of the individual provincial churches, and this assurance could not be obtained. The Eastern Church was approached in this, too, but the efforts in vain, as were those also with the Anglican Church. (This latter Church, Rome has decided, did not have valid orders.) The orders this Church was prepared to confer depended upon swearing an oath of allegiance to the English king. What complications that would have had in Hitler's Reich!

After much ado, a way was finally discovered of obtaining orders, and with them, of ranking in the apostolic succession. The friendly offer of assistance from a Gallican church, which traces its spiritual genealogy back to the Syro-Jacobite patriarchate of Antioch, came to the rescue of the High Church Union. The transcript of the genealogical tree which I possess shows that the pedigree begins with Mar Ignatius Peter III, the 144th successor of St. Peter. This Ignatius flourished about 1870.[5]

Professor Heiler of Marburg an der Lahn, who was president of the High Church Union, was chiefly responsible for discovering this solution. On August 25, 1930, he received, after all the usual minor orders, episcopal consecration at the hands of the bishop of the Gallican Church of the South of France, Petrus Gaston Vigué, assisted by two bishops. The *Rituale Romanum* was used.

Shortly before the High Church Congress in Berlin in October, 1930, Professor Heiler proceeded to confer orders himself. I was the first to be ordained. Although every precaution had been taken to keep these ordinations secret, the "Evangelical League for the Protection of German Evangelical Interests" got wind of it. The result was an unpleasant quarrel in the German church newspapers. But none of the church authorities ventured to raise objections to the fact that clergy under their jurisdiction had received the orders.

---

[5] [On this matter the reader is referred to E. C. Messenger, *The Reformation, the Mass, and the Priesthood* (New York, 1936-37), I, 229; II, 747-8.— *Pub.*]

In any case, they scarcely knew the names of those ordained, because there were only four of them. But from the standpoint of church history, it was important that there were now Protestant clergy who were not apostates from the Roman Catholic Church, but were genuine priests.

Efforts to build up a High-Church parish

The newly-ordained priests felt it their duty to quietly awaken, as the circumstances permitted, High-Church life in their parishes. I had the good fortune, shortly after my ordination, to take up a new post. This was the industrial town of Crimmitschau which is near Zwickau in Saxony. The church of St. John the Evangelist, only twenty years old, was entrusted to me. With the words, "My first gift to you is the gospel," I greeted my new parish on the Second Sunday after Easter, April 19, 1931. I knew that in time, I should speak of a second gift, but I had to proceed carefully.

Each year during autumn, I gave a series of lectures to my parishioners. I wanted to introduce my flock quite systematically to the life of faith. Six lectures on the Apostles' Creed which I had already delivered in Bad Schandau made a beginning. I followed these up with about twenty-five lectures on Holy Scripture, the nature of the sacraments and our need for them. I was very pleased by the number of people who attended these lectures. Members of the other two Evangelical Lutheran parishes in the town also came. The rise of National Socialist Movement made it necessary for me to speak on marriage, the family, and the nation, as well as on prayer and the need for confession. There was excitement when marriage was designated a sacrament and declared indissoluble, and when divorce was condemned. Finally, I brought the problem of the real meaning of the divine service to the fore. The mystery of the Church's existence was stressed. Thus, little by little we arrived at the Augsburg Confession and its most significant articles. All this occurred in the years before 1937. I invited a small circle of interested parishioners to study with me the Creed of the Evangelical Lutheran Church. Out of this there developed quite voluntarily, and without formal association with the High Church Union, a High Church group. In this group we discovered the articles of the Augsburg Confession which treat of the Mass. With astonishment we read the words, "Retinetur missa apud nos et summa reverentia celebratur" ("The Mass will be retained among us and celebrated with the utmost reverence"). That was Lutheranism! Once this was understood, I announced the first High Church service for a Sunday evening in Advent.

Then the words were spoken, "My second gift is the 'German Mass,' which I bring you today." A certain amount of courage was necessary to appear all of a sudden before the altar vested for Mass. I still remember how I hesitated behind the altar before I strode round it. But it had to be dared. The number of those present was small. They came from among the parishioners I had gathered together and upon whose understanding I thought I could depend. They were properly prepared. Nothing had been unduly hurried. It would have been remarkable if a lasting impression had not been made upon these faithful ones, to whom I still feel grateful, who expressed a desire for further services of a like nature. Thus the way was cleared and a nucleus of High Church life was formed. A side chapel near the beautiful sacristy of our church has a small altar which seemed to be designed to hold a tabernacle. This now received the Holy Eucharist under the form of bread, and a sanctuary lamp now burned for the first time in an Evangelical Church in honor of the Lord. It was easy to pray there. In the "Motherland of the Reformation" a springtime of devotion had begun which was about to bring forth other blossoms.

It almost goes without saying that the parish was also drawn to love the Mother of God. One of the panels of the splendid altarpiece in the church had a statue of our Lady standing with St. John at the foot of the cross. The liturgy of the Lutheran Church in Saxony had retained three feasts of our Lady, the Purification, the Annunciation, and the Visitation, together with their respective lessons and prayers. One had only to adhere to the old liturgy in order to put new life into the feast days. Furthermore, there are good grounds for the celebration of the feasts of the Blessed Virgin Mary in the *Apology for the Augsburg Confession* (art. 21, 27). There one reads, "Maria orat pro ecclesia" ("Mary prays for the Church"), and the Mother of God is spoken of as *dignissima amplissimis honoribus* ("most worthy of the highest honors"). But what Protestant Church is true to its confessional writings or, if these are not in high favor, to the New Testament where in Luke 1:48 we read, "Behold, from this day forward all generations shall call me blessed"? A church which does not honor Mary is unworthy of her Son. The difficulty of making this plausible to my parish can be imagined.

Thus, with a good conscience and with the approval of the faithful, these venerable old feasts were celebrated once more, and in appropriate liturgical vestments. The rochet and stole were used for Matins and Vespers. The Matins of the great feasts, which took place early in the morning, were followed by the celebration of the Eucharist with all the pomp of the Church. On the evening of Holy Saturday, the Easter feast began according to a rite worked out by the Berneuchenern. There was a Paschal candle and the blessing of the baptismal water. Everything which makes the Easter eve so great was included in the splendid ceremony which was public and could be attended by anyone of good will. In any case, the main body of the participants had been sufficiently prepared and were quite familiar with both the hymns and the ritual.

Hitler's war cast a blight upon this brave endeavor as it did upon others. I got into difficulties with the Gestapo like all the other clergymen who were unable to go the way of the "German Christians." We were subjected to house-searching, supervision of religious services, etc. The "German Christians" had a strong supporter in the chief burgomaster of the city of Crimmitschau, which lies close to the Thuringian border, and was therefore predestined to be the gate through which Thuringia was invaded. This burgomaster had managed to place himself at the head of the Kirchgemeindeverbande [6] and was, although a German Christian, leader of the local Gestapo as well. This is how the Protestant Church was abused. On account of my High

---

[6] That is, the union of the parishes in the area.

Church tendencies, I was suspected of being "on my way to Rome," and I was obliged to curtail my activities considerably.

The German Christians and the state church

I shall content myself with a few short remarks on this subject. These people, who almost became the gravediggers of the Protestant Church, were at first protected by the National Socialist Party but later, like all the rest, fell under suspicion. They had their stronghold at the center for the regional Church in Dresden. This center ruled over our churches for the advantage of their fellow German Christians. Our churches were commandeered for the special events of the German Christians without the permission of the parishes. The "Reichsbischof," Ludwig Müller, visited our town to baptize children there. Bishop Peter of Berlin, Leutheuser, and other leading personalities had to contribute to the consolidation of the German Christians of Crimmitschau. A German Christian clergyman holding high office in Dresden instituted (this is the only possible word) a "baptism" in my church. I looked on from the sacristy. This gentleman arbitrarily altered the baptismal formula, and he tore to pieces the belief in the Holy Trinity. His formula went something like this, "I baptize thee in the name of the all-loving Father, and of the Son and in His spirit." I challenged him about his heretical formula, but he was too cowardly to explain himself clearly. I was forced, however, to enter this "baptism" in the register, but I added the marginal note, "This child was not baptized in accordance with

Matt. 28:10." This did not in any way upset the superintendent who inspected the register later. These gentlemen
had burned their bridges behind them. All that remained
was the New Testament which was very much abbreviated,
and the sacraments that were meaningless appendages to
their "God Festivals."

It was a terrible, agonizing period of decline. With the
break-up of the Third Reich, things improved, at least out-
wardly. But liberalism was not dead. Unity of doctrine has
never been attained, and it is open to anyone to believe
what he will and to make his own religion. This is also true
of the clergy of the Protestant Church. Anyone who has
studied the efforts made by Protestants to create a unified
Evangelical Church of Germany knows how irreconcilable
are the differences within this Church.

In spite of my leaving the Protestant Church, which incident I will recount later, I have continued to take considerable interest in the development of the Evangelical Church
in Germany. I know that people are making sincere efforts in
many ways, such as rejecting the Bultmann tendencies,
and making the marriage of divorced persons impossible.
But how can they succeed in this latter effort when they do
not recognize marriage as a sacrament?

"Catholic" and "Roman"—various Protestant standpoints

However welcome are the proposals for a new liturgy for
the use of the various Evangelical Lutheran "member"
Churches within the United Evangelical Lutheran Church

of Germany, it is a matter for thought that within the member Churches voices are being raised that strongly object to such proposals as being far too "Catholic." What is to become of the efforts of the High Church Union which wants to go very much further in a "Catholic" direction? They will continue to draw opposition. Moreover, there are those who are enemies of all the efforts to improve church services which go beyond the "simplicity" of a preaching service. Because there are so many of these contrary tendencies at work, progress, or regeneration is out of the question. As it became increasingly clear that I could no longer believe in this possibility, I arrived at the inevitable conclusion.

The question now arises concerning the High Church Union's approval of such a step. Does the High Church Union want a fusion, does it want to be united with Rome? The answer to this is that the Union certainly wants to be Catholic in its own way, but not Roman. Like the Augsburg Confession, it makes the traditional distinction between Catholic and Roman.[7] In the High Church Union it was an unwritten law that no one should so much as express the idea of being converted. It was felt that it would not only be disloyal, but that it would serve neither the Protestant nor the Roman Catholic Church. For it was the intention of the Union to aid not only the Protestant Church, but through its influence, however small, to win Rome over. This organization wanted to persuade the Catholic Church to abandon what was considered a rigid juridical system and to develop gradually from a "legalistic Church" (Rechtskirche)

[7] Cf. the summary following the twenty-first Article in the Müller-Kolde edition of the Augsburg Confession.

into a "Johannine" Church. It was believed that when these modifications were thoroughly worked out that the Protestant Church could find a place therein. The general opinion has been that anyone who goes over to Rome is like a drop of water that falls into the sea and which is absorbed without having the slightest effect.

After the war

Immediately after the liberation of our town from the Nazi yoke, the rule of the German Christians came to an end. The enormous swastika was hauled down from the roof of the Martin Luther Church in Crimmitschau, hitherto the stronghold of the German Christians. The "God Feasts" were finished. I thought it a favorable moment to openly suggest the "German Mass" as the parish service, and I celebrated it in this form on Sundays and Wednesdays. On Wednesdays, I always wore the chasuble. I began to lecture again and it was easy to show, in the distorted efforts of the German Christians who were so closely tied with National Socialism, what danger had threatened the Lutheran Church: nothing short of destruction.

Saxony was at first split up into a Russian and a small American zone of occupation. Crimmitschau belonged to the latter. Since Dresden was in the Russian zone of occupation and inaccessible to us, we had no consistorial connections and consequently led a completely free ecclesiastical existence. This situation changed when West Saxony, too, was finally handed over to the Soviet occupation forces. Pastors of the Confessional Church took the helm and filled the high positions in the provincial office for Church affairs. Subsequently, they had their authority confirmed by a synod.

Since I was the oldest member of the High Church Union living in the Eastern zone, I was entrusted by Professor Heiler with the leadership of a meeting of the members of the Union in East Germany. So, in 1949, I invited any friends and acquaintances who had survived the war to a High Church Congress in Crimmitschau. The Congress was to have arrangements similar to the *Una Sancta* meetings. With the knowledge and approval of the Archbishop of Paderborn, two priests from Magdeburg also took part, one of whom made a report. The theme chosen was the "Holy Sacraments" and it treated of those which the present-day Evangelical Lutheran Church does not recognize as such. During this High Church Congress, confirmation and holy orders were conferred. At the solemn high Mass which concluded the Congress, a considerable number of the laity from the town were present. However, my local colleagues, who held views very different from mine, were present at none of the meetings and were, in any case, not invited. This congress had an important sequel.

Apostolic Succession and Lutheranism

The fact that some of my brethren in the High Church Union had received holy orders stirred up a good deal of discussion. A group of students who used to meet annually at the end of the school year in a little town in the Erz Gebirge was heard discussing the subject. It was said that holy orders were being conferred upon Protestant clergy by Roman Catholic priests. How abysmal is the ignorance that gives rise to such absurd ideas!

There was a conference for the clergy in Leipzig, and one of the ministers asked the administrative head of the office of the regional Church of Dresden, Licentiate Noth (now provincial bishop), if, in his position in the provincial Church office, he was aware of what had happened in Crimmitschau. Consequently, the office was obliged to send me a very formal and official document, dated August 3, 1949. This informed me that to undertake priestly orders was not compatible with either the beliefs or the wishes of the provincial Church and was therefore expressly forbidden. At the same time I was notified of a "discussion" to be held in Dresden, the object of which was to clarify the very serious problems which had arisen as a result of my activities.

This meeting took place on October 24, 1949, and I was well aware that things would go against me. These gentlemen had their instructions. The main point on the agenda was the significance and justification of the Apostolic Succession, especially within the Protestant and, above all, the Lutheran Church. In this context other things were considered, such as the necessity of ordination, the doctrine of the sacraments with special emphasis on the Eucharist. I submitted the following points:

1. My ordination in the provincial Church was too uncertain because it did not rest upon the Apostolic Succession; the chain beginning with the apostles had been broken as a result of the Reformation.

2. Lutheran confessional documents clearly indicated

that the Succession was to be retained under certain conditions.

3. The Protestant ecumenical movement obviously required the Succession.

4. Intercommunion with the non-German Evangelical Churches would be possible only if the principle of Apostolic Succession were accepted. (The absence of this intercommunion at the great Church congresses had been very distressing.)

5. Justice required that the High Church should be allowed to confer holy orders, since this right had been granted to the Berneucheners for their members.[8] After all ordination is restricted to members of our Brotherhood and conferred only on those who seek it.

At this point, the following should be noted. Shortly before the induction of the provincial bishop, Hahn, which took place in the cathedral of Meissen, two representatives of the High Church Union (which had recently changed its name to the Evangelical Ecumenical Circle) had presented a document for episcopal approval which contained the purposes and principles of the movement. In a letter of response the bishop had shown a truly fatherly interest in them, and had agreed to take their efforts to restore the ancient church order and the Apostolic Succession very seriously, and endeavor to gain a more intimate knowledge of

---

8 This movement is in many ways similar to the High Church Union. It has managed to obtain recognition from various provincial churches (e.g., in Hanover) because, unlike the High Church Union, it has been very restrained in its demands. But it seems to me that it is developing in a manner similar to the High Church Union.

the subject, which was new to him. After seeing the rules of the Brotherhood of the Evangelical Ecumenical Circle, he said that he would never interfere in the internal affairs of this group.

During my theological studies, I had never even heard of the Apostolic Succession. Later on I was to learn that my colleagues, to whom I referred the subject, were quite unaware of it, and showed little interest in the subject. Thus it is not surprising that at the Dresden "discussion," no one knew what I was talking about, and so no progress could be made.

I therefore took the liberty of referring them to the confessional documents of the Evangelical Lutheran Church and pointed out to the gentlemen the following facts: In the Augsburg Confession, article 14, it is stated that no one shall teach publicly in the Church or administer the sacraments who is not *rite vocatus,* "lawfully called." And in Article 28 of the same document it is written that the episcopal authority to preach and administer the sacraments, including holy orders, is *de jure divino,* "by divine right." Moreover, in the Apology for the Augsburg Confession, Article 13, 11, there is the following passage, "Si autem ordo de ministerio verbi intelligatur, non gravatim vocaverimus ordinem sacramentum" ("But if a decision is to be given concerning the nature of ministry of the World, we should unhesitatingly call it a sacrament").

What I considered to be the most convincing piece of evidence was the following passage which I quoted from that section of the Apology which deals with Article 14 of the **Augsburg Confession:**

"De ordina ecclesiastico: Articulum in quo dicimus 'nemini nisi rite vocato' concedendum esse administrationem sacramentorum et verbi in ecclesia, ita recipiunt, si tamen utimur ordinatione canonica. Hac de re in hoc conventu saepe testati sumus, nos summa voluntate cupere conservare politiam ecclesiasticam et gradus in ecclesia factos etiam humana auctoritate. Scimus enim bono et utili consilio a patribus ecclesiasticam disciplinam hoc modo, ut veteres canones describunt, constitutam esse. . . . Porro hoc iterum volumus testatum, nos libenter conservaturos esse ecclesiasticam et canonicam politiam, si modo episcopi desinant in nostras ecclesias saevire."

"Our opponents allow our article 14, in which we say that no one ought to have the administration of the word and the sacraments in the Church unless he be rightly called, on condition that we make use of canonical ordination. On this point we several times pointed out in the Diet that we most earnestly desired to retain the ecclesiastical polity and the grades in the Church, even those made by human authority. For we know that it was with good and useful counsel that ecclesiastical discipline, as the ancient canons describe, was constituted by the fathers. For this reason we say again, that we will most willingly help conserve the ecclesiastical and canonical polity, if only the bishops will desist raging in our churches."

That which the confessors of Augsburg rejected, therefore, was simply canonical obedience to bishops who suppress their teaching the gospel and the Word of God. The venerable and canonical system of holy orders and, with it, the Apostolic Succession they hold in the highest honor.

"Brethren, be worthy of your fathers!" But for centuries, the sons of those fathers have been unwilling to respect and observe the canonical order which has been forgotten or fallen into disrepute. That was a tradition too. Would the return have been a mere restoration of the original order or no real return to the source after all?

My quotations from the confessional document had no effect. They were quickly thrown aside. These quotations of mine represented concessions that were made by the confessors. They did little good because the Roman Catholic Church remained inflexible. This is a fine example of what must happen when one negotiates. The obligation, which one accepted on ordination, to teach in accordance with the confessional documents does not bind when it comes to things that were once historical facts, but are not true today. Deviation from such a tenuous commitment should not be surprising.

If the reader will bear with me, I should like to break off my narrative in order to insert a few important points relative to holy orders. It is interesting to question non-German Lutheran Churches concerning their attitude in this matter. The Church of Sweden holds firmly to the traditional consecration of bishops and priests, and this on the grounds of Apostolic Succession. For them, the Augsburg Confession would be binding. The following are the words of Archbishop Söderblom, "As we affirmed at the Anglo-Swedish conference in Upsala in 1919, we look upon the particular forms and traditions of our Church, not merely with the reverence due to a venerable inheritance from our fathers, but as a gift entrusted to us by the God of history.

The value of the episcopacy was emphasized by Laurentius Petri in his Church Discipline of 1571, 'Therefore, because this law was extremely useful and doubtless came from God in the person of the Holy Spirit, the giver of all good gifts, it was accepted and approved throughout Christendom, and has persisted ever since, and must continue to exist as long as the world lasts, notwithstanding the many abuses to which it has been subject (as are all other blessed and valuable things from time to time); which abuses must be abolished.' And in our section of the Church, there is no room for the least doubt concerning the unbroken continuity of what has been called the Apostolic Succession."

A Swedish friend of the High Church Union, Dr. Gunnar Rosendal, professor of theology at Osby, writing on August 26, 1949, said that he could not understand his Protestant brethren in Germany who contend that the Apostolic Succession is contrary to the Augsburg Confession. His view is that, without the Succession, it is by no means certain that, apart from baptism, there are any sacraments at all. He emphasized further that the Swedish Church teaches the *character indelebilis,* the indelible stamp of priestly ordination. Non-German Protestant Churches (as in England) have kept the old orders, but the German Protestant Church has given them all up, and the entire German Evangelical Church thus lacks proper leadership.

At the meeting, our consideration of the Apostolic Succession and what it meant for the Church in general, for the Church's worship, its total activity, and its relationship with sister Churches, led imperceptibly but inevitably to the question of the administration of the sacraments. I believed

I was defending a good cause when I reported that in my parish great value was laid upon the celebration of the Lord's Supper, as was proved by the mounting numbers of communicants, which were high in comparison with those of the two other Lutheran churches in Crimmitschau. Statistics were available. Their argument against me was that by using additional prayers at this celebration, by changing the liturgy, and by employing ancient ecclesiastical vestments I had brought confusion into the town and its parishes and that this was "upsetting." That is how the provincial bishop expressed it. A provincial Church councilor completed this statement by saying that the number of communicants was of purely negative value!

These words struck me like a thunderbolt. At that moment my whole future was decided. It became quite clear to me that I could not and should not belong any longer to this Church which could thus undervalue, without any basis in reason or tradition, the sincere efforts of one of its clergymen to give the proper form to its highest celebration, and to win men to believe in and use the sacraments. The realization was painful. The "discussion" ended with the result that the Evangelical Protestant clergy were forbidden to have themselves ordained in a High-Church manner or to wear the vestments of ancient tradition.

It was at this point that my conversion to Catholicism began. Yet, more than two years were to pass before I finally broke away. Since I was observed as being so "Catholic," it would be worth while to subject to careful scrutiny those who, it is true, perform the liturgy in the prescribed manner or shorten it somewhat, but how deny important revealed truths (such as the Virgin Birth, the Resurrection, and so on). According to Bishop Dibelius in Berlin, speaking to the members of the Evangelical Ecumenical Circle, one might, of course, believe anything that one could conscientiously defend as being consonant with the Protestant Church as a whole, but one was not permitted to do anything to the order of the provincial Church. (By this he meant the provincial church ordination.)

If preaching in the Protestant Church is entirely free as is claimed, it surely follows that one is free to test by Holy Scripture the orders of the provincial Church. If, as a result of this, one comes to the conclusion that these orders as they exist are not in accordance with the inspired Word of God, then one should be permitted to say so openly. Furthermore, any individual or group ought to be permitted, by taking appropriate action, to offer practical help to the provincial Church, as the High Church Union did, in order to remedy this faulty development. This is not destructive criticism. It is a mode of procedure springing directly from the very nature of the Protestant Church and is, in addition, an act of charity.

The future of the Protestant Church: May one hope or ought one to remain skeptical?

The Protestant Church is a conglomeration of the most varied views and currents of thought. It is true that the storms of the Hitler period have been weathered, but it became obvious during that period that destructive forces were at work within it. Where did the large number of German

Christians come from so suddenly, who, as one of their leading figures remarked, rejected all dogma and started again
from the "beginning." An opposite trend can be seen in the
ranks of the Confessing Church (*Bekennende Kirche*)—not
the Confessional Church (*Bekenntnis Kirche*)—because people
are not unwilling to listen today to Karl Barth, and they cannot get rid of Bultmann's ideas. As members of the Confessing Church, Karl Barth and Bultmann were, of course, bitter
opponents of the National Socialist Party with which the
German Christians were in sympathy.

A document dating from the period just previous to
World War I throws some light on the situation in the
Protestant Church. I should like to refer to it here. In the
process of working upon the present account, I came across
a book of sermons by Professor Schlatter whom I had heard
preach in Tübingen. In a sermon delivered on Reformation
Sunday, he spoke as follows: "We ought today to think of the
Reformation with solemn joy and gratitude. Have we the
courage to do so? Of course, when we think of the bad, dark
things of which the Reformation rid us, of the pope, the
monks, the confessional, the Mass and so on, we are glad this
yoke was taken from us; . . . but when we look at our Protestant people today one fact is obvious: they are falling off!
And the proof of this lies in the fact that our Protestant
churches are crumbling." He then goes on to speak of the
causes as he saw them then, points the way to improvement,
and finally sums up, "For our fathers, everything was based
on belief. They wanted to trust God, be certain of God, take
a firm grip on Jesus' hand, and remain His in life and death.
It was for that reason that they dismissed the pope, broke up

the confessional, and tore up their monk's habit. They wanted to believe, and these things were hindrances to belief; they threw away everything which stood in the way of their faith."

Schlatter had here described the situation of the Protestant Church with frankness and clarity. He was far too objective not to see the decline. Moreover, there is still plenty of evidence of that, as becomes daily more obvious. The Evangelical Lutheran Church still holds in reverence the Apostles' Creed, which it divides into three well-known articles; the second article concerning the divine Redeemer and the third concerning the Holy Ghost offer so much that is positive that one can build very successfully upon them. But why does one never preach upon the theme, "Born of the Virgin Mary" in the light of the historical veracity of the text from St. Luke, chapters one and two? What great spiritual value could be derived from an explanation of the angelic salutation alone, "The Lord is with thee"!

One has only to consider that God is with Mary, not merely in the moment of being greeted, but that He, the Eternal, unbound to time, was already at all times with her, and in that moment, too, when the physical life of the Mother of God took its origin, and she was preserved from the stain of Original Sin. The humble human being then comes quite spontaneously to the worship of God and reverence for Mary, whom the Lord has distinguished as the first of all creatures on account of her dignity as the Mother of God.

There is true substance, too, in the splendid hymns of the Protestant Church, especially in those that come from the early period. Words and melodies are so uplifting that no small number could be taken over untouched by the Catholic Church. The new Evangelical Unity-Hymnbook is full of the fundamental truths of the faith and true Christian piety. However, many treasures of music have not found acceptance, and these must be newly discovered and distributed. We want to call the attention of our separated brethren to these.

In Protestant circles, it seems necessary, even if at first only among small groups, that, in order to end the division, the cord must be joined at the point at which it broke. Efforts are being made to restore confession even if unaccompanied by the confessional box. People are longing for the Mass. There are even voices raised in praise of the cloister. The beginnings of this work were already apparent when the press reported that Pastor Gunnar Rosendal in Osby (mentioned above), had consecrated a young woman as a nun without the knowledge of his ecclesiastical superiors and had, as a result, incurred their displeasure. He declared that it was his intention to found a Lutheran Evangelical order of nuns. Pastor Rosendal assured me that the press report was correct but added with great emphasis, "I could never become a *Roman* Catholic! The new dogmas render that impossible." That was intended as his reply to my letter telling him of my conversion. The community of the "Brothers of the Common Life," of whom I heard in the spring of 1954 at a meeting of members of the *Una Sancta* circle, has as one of its aims a conventual settlement, too. Furthermore, a small cloistered community has already started its life on Calvinist soil at the

German-Swiss frontier. Are these only the expressions of a romantic enthusiasm, or is there more behind them?

There is no lack of welcome signs of life. That is true. Yet so long as the anti-Roman attitude is maintained, hopes of a reunion are utopian. In the decisive moment, it seems that Protestantism will allow itself to be led by that spirit to which Professor Hermelink of Marburg gave expression, "As a Protestant, it is my business and my lot in the historic function of Protestantism to offer protest, and, in the name of that God who reveals Himself as mercy and judgment in my conscience where by His Word He gives me justifying faith, to oppose all world manifestations of Catholicism either inside the Roman Church or outside it in Protestant Churches or sects." Professor Karl Heim of Tübingen has expressed himself similarly.

What I want to say is that from a psychological standpoint people in Protestant and Lutheran circles are afraid to approach God too closely. It is for this reason that they will hear nothing of a Real Change taking place in Holy Mass. Belief in the Incarnation and in the Real Presence in the Holy Eucharist is lacking. A Leipzig professor, belonging to the *Berneuchenern,* gave his judgment at a conference of St. Michael's Brotherhood at which I was present. He said, in passing, that the Protestant was certainly looking for God, but that he finds too close a contact with God distasteful (*unsympathisch*)! How very different does the joyful teaching of Deut. 4:7 sound in the mouth of St. Thomas, *Neque enim est aut fuit aliquando tam grandis natio, quae habeat deos appropinquantes sibi, sicut adest nobis Deus noster* ("For there is not, and there never was, any nation so blessed as to have their gods so close to them the way our God is close to us"). But the Protestant theologians do not esteem Thomas too highly.

Introibo ad altare Dei

I gave up my post in Crimmitschau on April 1, 1952. After a long period of instruction and waiting, the auxiliary bishop for Magdeburg in the Archdiocese of Paderborn, the Very Reverend Friedrich Rintelen, ordained me in the old and venerable abbey of Huysburg near Halberstadt on December 19, 1953. On December 27, I celebrated my first Mass in the church of St. Mary in Köthen (Anhalt). This church has had a memorable history. More than one hundred years ago it was built by Duke Ferdinand and his wife, Julie of Köthen-Anhalt, when these two became Catholics—to the great horror of the Protestant world at that time, of their relations, and of the population of the small duchy. These rulers rest in the crypt beneath the high altar of the church, where they are still remembered annually at Mass. And now a former Protestant pastor is permitted to stand and celebrate at this altar.

People have often asked me what has become of the parish that I educated in High-Church ways. Unfortunately, I am forced to reply, "It has disappeared." Some of its members have found their way into the Mother Church, but the majority have remained what they were, or have become again what they formerly were. The High-Church clergy have no *successio personalis*, they are not followed by men of like mind who continue the work they have begun. This is painful. A former colleague, who, without being a member of the High Church Union, works along High-Church lines in his parish in the Hanover province, once wrote to me as follows, "When I leave this place, my parishioners will have to live once again on semiliberal sermons and improvised prayer."

This statement sums up the fate of most of the parishes run on High-Church lines. My former friends work on conscientiously in silence, but they usually have to be satisfied with giving very modest stimulation. They have to remain patiently in the background, especially since, in the territory of the East German Democratic Republic, the Church authorities have more or less plainly condemned High Church efforts and warned the clergy. Unfortunately, so far as I can gather, none of my former friends shows any desire to emerge from his ambiguous position and go where I have gone. They think they can be satisfied with the reception of ordination in the Evangelical Ecumenical Circle and have become to a certain extent immune to further insights and consequences. They remain in no man's land between opposing camps. But the fact that one cannot at the same time be an ordained priest and Protestant pastor of the provincial Church creates a critical situation.

By God's grace I have been permitted to overcome this difficulty and am happy and grateful to be a Catholic priest. I was granted a particularly sacred and personally significant privilege when, on July 26, 1955, a day after the consecration of the former provost of Leipzig, Dr. Otto Spülbeck, as coadjutor bishop of Meissen, which took place in St. Peter's

Cathedral in Bautzen, I was able to approach the high altar there and celebrate before the faithful, very few of whom guessed the significance of the occasion, my first Mass "at home." From the font in the Protestant part of the cathedral to the high altar in the Catholic part—a long way, but one blessed with many graces. *Deo gratias!*

Some final thoughts

I still see myself as I stood as a choir boy in the choir loft of the church of my baptism, the lofty Cathedral of St. Peter at Bautzen. In the right aisle is the altar of the Protestant parish; in the middle of the vast church, the Lutheran pulpit; and behind, in the chancel, in the apse, the great high altar of the Roman Catholic congregation, with its painting of St. Peter receiving the keys of heaven from our Lord's hands. Before it, there glows the mysterious, perpetually burning sanctuary lamp, signifying that silence and devotion must reign in this place, where Christ has pitched His tent. But between the sections there was a grating which separates, with the harsh reality of iron, the two confessions. Of course, the grating has been there since 1564, but the spatial separation it emphasizes is a significant symbol of a far more profound inward separation.

Thus, one stands in thought before it. To what sincere Christian, who is fully conscious of the meaning of the all-embracing love of the divine Saviour, would this question not occur: Why the grating? And if men are silent, the stones of which the cathedral is built shout it out; as our Lord said, "I tell you that if these keep silence, the stones will cry out"

(Luke 19:40). But at this time, the persecution under which many Christians live shouts it, and neither do we know when that suffering will descend aggressively upon us again. This distress cries out, "You have but one Master, and you are all brothers" (Matt. 23:8).

And so we must pray the words our Lord Himself gave us to petition the Father, "Forgive us our trespasses as we forgive those that trespass against us."

The medieval Church had been to blame in many respects, popular Protestantism never tires of repeating these failings. To some extent this "work" is its life principle. Because of the fact that the last German pope, Adrian VI (1522-23), who, unfortunately, had ascended the chair of Peter too late, had in all candor admitted this fault, and because distinguished historians of the Roman Catholic Church have admitted the guilt, there is plenty of evidence that we on our side should repeat the request of the Our Father, "Forgive us our trespasses." But what about the other side?

But during the century of the Reformation, more was probably at stake than opening the eyes of a blind clergy to the abuses which Hadrian named so frankly. Other and more serious issues were involved. The "ecumenical" Luther, whom the whole Church might call her own, is not revealed in his controversial writings which smoke with his anger. But a broader perception of Luther can be recognized in his struggle for the assurance of a sin-forgiving grace. "With a bold hand, Luther seizes the highest thing, snatches it from the fullness of Catholic life, and places it upon a lonely throne." [9] Luther's deed after his "tower experience" may be

9 Heiler, *Im Ringen um die Kirche*, p. 213.

characterized in some such manner. Why? Because, following his individual predispositions he had seized upon that which suited him personally. When he had gone so far, an enormous simplification became necessary. The whole Catholic system, the essence of which is fullness, universality, diversity, and freedom from one-sidedness, had to bend in the face of this simplification. It is true that he found at hand a few isolated stones of the gigantic Catholic cathedral which could be easily refashioned and fitted into his simple Evangelical temple, but the system as a whole could not be recast.[10] Was this God's guidance and will? Father Böminghaus, S.J., says, "Why should we not regard it as possible that Luther was called within the Catholic Church to the task of not only stemming decay but of bringing light from the inexhaustible depths of the Christian Catholic faith new treasures, and of stamping with his own rich life new features of Christian piety? He probably had this task, but his task of serving the whole, the universal Church, went to pieces upon his own temperament and that of his opponent, and so the Church which identified itself with him became a sect." But why after more than four hundred years, must millions still suffer the hard fate of separation and not even be aware of the evil?

Luther's immense simplification, however, led inevitably to an unparalleled impoverishment, to a stunted growth, to a spiritual dissipation, which the simple man in the street fails to understand but which leads him straight into a sort of spiritual nihilism. Along with it there goes a pharisaism, perhaps unconscious, which has brought into existence innum-

[10] *Ibid.,* p. 230.

erable Protestant denominations and factions. And all claim that they are right. They all have indeed fragments of the truth, but never the whole.

An individual, even when he is a great man and his fervor cannot be challenged, is in no position to grasp the complete fullness of the Church. But a human being cannot live away from this fullness in an isolated corner, however splendid it is. He has need of the influx of power that comes from the fullness. St. Paul, the Apostle of the Gentiles, speaks of this when in his First Epistle to the Corinthians, he makes his striking comments upon the variety of the separate members of the human body. For each member, to each organ, there is an appropriate dignity, and none of them may glorify itself beyond the other. Together, they produce completeness; together, they guarantee the body's life. Thus is it also in the Church. No particular doctrine withdrawn from the rest is fullness, but is simply a part, and can only be effective along with the other parts.

Behind Luther there stood the inspired Word of the Bible, which to him was all important; for any Christian it is all-important, wherever he is. But Luther saw it in his own particular, individual situation, in his one-sidedness. So he lost the ability to see the other things in the Church. Furthermore, he read from his Bible only those things which seemed to him important and put other things aside. Thus, among other things, he overlooked the breadth of the Church whose character is a great synthesis in which the natural and the supernatural integrate like the wheels of an intricate piece of clockwork.[11] For she has harmonized and balanced all antith-

11 Cf. *Ibid.*, p. 210.

esis. She was flexible enough to absorb and assimilate the finest elements in other religions, without being unfaithful to Him who founded her. She has in this manner accepted from the beginning much that Luther, for example, condemned as heathen. In spite of everything, however, the Church has adhered to the known truth by being able to hold in balance the things of the spirit and those of the world. She was, and is, of divine origin, and is the mother of mankind.

Can this be said of the various splinter churches? Have they this breadth? Why do Protestants feel that they interpret the Word of God more successfully and have it more completely than others when, in fact, the dubious "success" of poorly attended services shows that vast numbers of those who live in predominantly Protestant areas no longer hear or desire to hear the Word! If the teaching Church preaches the Word unceasingly it ought to see the faithful gathered in crowds around its pulpits. But where are they? That they are not there is eloquent testimony. And why are the people tired of all the talking? "Forgive us our trespasses." This is echoed in the acknowledgment of Adrian VI and in numerous writings of other Catholics. It is also heard from the mouths of Protestants. But for a long time now we have been familiar with that other expression, without which we can make no progress, the sincere belief of which the Lord of the Church is waiting, before He can help us, "As we forgive those who trespass against us." High-minded men, Protestant and Catholic clergy and laity are extending to one another the hand of friendship. They do not overlook the ditches that have been dug but seek to bridge them over by obeying the commandment to love. But most of them still stick to their preconceived opinions, not comprehending the seriousness of the situation. My brothers, the situation is serious! May God help us!

In the cathedral of my native town the hymn *Ein feste Burg ist unser Gott,* "A Mighty Fortress is Our God," is still sung; and at another hour, on the other side of the grating, are heard the joyous words of the pontifical Mass, *Gaudeamus omnes in Domino, diem festum celebrantes sub honore sanctorum,* "Let us all rejoice in the Lord, celebrating a feast day in honor of the saints."

However, between the choirs in song and the congregations, between the pealing jubilant organs, there stands a grating.

Thou, O Lord, hast prayed that all may be one; and we have separated.

GEORG KLÜNDER

The Church Is Fullness

AFTER MANY YEARS in which I have constantly tested the theological principles and the ecclesiastical and practical situation in the Protestant Church, I have decided to renounce my office in that Church and to become a Catholic.

You, my greatly respected and dear brethren, should not be particularly surprised at this news. You heard in the ecclesiastical councils the tenor of my criticism of developments in the provincial Churches. You are aware of my vigorous complaints in regard to the liberty with which individual ministers work up attitudes of protests which are often of a very narrow significance; you know the disorder consequent upon such behavior and its toleration by the authorities; and you know my attitude toward the inner problems which have marked the spiritual situation of German Protestantism, in particular, for many years and which underlie the present obstacles. You share my knowledge and more than once you have been involved in the manifold difficulties I have had in making contact with the leaders of the Evangelical Church, with the object of protecting the unalterable demands of the Church's honor and dignity. The constant harassment of making multitudinous agreements, often born of a mere momentary situation, was at times so great that the negative aspect of my position overshadowed my real vocation of pastoral solicitude, which in itself can justify the decisive step I have taken. There were indeed plenty of discussions of principles at our meetings, but the clashes with the practical reality of the Protestant Church were always in the forefront. Thus it is possible for the impression to arise that I left only as a result of sheer irritation. Further, one might also ask, "Was there no way you could avoid the conflict and find a solution acceptable to all sides?" But there was no such way, because those problems lying behind the exterior, which have appeared superficial to you, are of a fundamental character. It is for this reason that I owe you a thorough discussion of the problems that were solved by my decision.

I am strengthened in this intention by the consideration of the spiritual reaction which my departure has sometimes provoked in you. Even if you wished to make up your minds intellectually, you found it harder to do so emotionally. I know that your brotherly feelings toward me continue; but at the same time you will inquire somewhat anxiously, "Was all that is past wrong, then? Are we still his brothers in Christ, or have we become pitiable creatures in his eyes? Or are we perhaps even enemies, whom he regards with the irreconcilable hostility of the renegade?"

These questions have a very special importance because my impact upon your lives was not merely a momentary one, for I was eighteen years in my first curacy so that, apart from the superintendent himself, I was in my church district longer than anyone else. I will not hide from you the fact that the break with my longstanding connections was painful, as are all partings in this life. You will gather from this statement that I shall not "burn what I previously worshiped," just as I did not "burn what I now adore"; these words were put into the mouth of the bishop of Reims by Gregory of Tours in the course of recounting the conversion of Chlodweg. They in no wise apply to the present relationship between the confessions, nor to any genuine conversion situation. Words like these dangerously simplify the complex character of the inner process of the mind and heart and give undue prominence to primitive or unessential motives. A conversion based upon such inadequate grounds should be avoided at all costs.

Let me make it plain to begin with, my brethren, that my decision is the result of a period of development that lasted for ten years. As you have participated in the last stage of this development, and, then, only on the margin of the field of final decision, my resolve must have appeared sudden, although, it did, in fact, develop gradually and without interruption. The explosive, precipitate, and the ecstatic are no signs of the Catholic religion, as I understand it; sudden conversions and excited enthusiasms have fundamentally very little to do with Catholicism. If it is ever possible to speak of an inner occurrence as having anything to do with a sudden break, it is something quite foreign to my religious development.

My first experience of the appeal of the ancient Catholic liturgy took place on October 31, 1922, when a "German Mass" was celebrated in the Protestant church of St. Nicholas in Berlin. It took place during an annual conference of the High Church Movement and was intended as an example of the Lutheran services of the sixteenth and seventeenth centuries. It left with me a deep aesthetic impression; a mixture of psalmody and incense seemed to billow within me. I was still young and quite susceptible to everything beautiful.

The world of visible beauty is not by any means an unessential constituent of Catholic fullness. It has a positive fitness in the whole pattern of Catholic oneness of life for it is a way in which, as creatures, we express our joy and thankfulness. The recognition that these tangible things of the world can be valid symbols of the divine, as well as prophetic indications of a future corporeal life makes us aware of the fullness of the wisdom of God that will be revealed in the next life as a new heaven and a new earth. When it is serviceably inclosed in the vast framework of church life, this aesthetic world of values mediates, maintains and promotes faith and love. But if it goes beyond this position of service, if it escapes from its inferior station, it may become a seducer among those who are susceptible. In itself it is not reason for a conversion, for it brings with it the dangerous appeal to make a decision before the experiential foundations in reason and faith are laid. Every tone is struck in the very rich scale of the emotions. Heart and soul are deeply inspired by the jubilation of Gregorian chant, the silent and awe-inspiring beauty of the cathedral, the solemn movement of a joyful procession, and the red glimmer of the perpetually burning light in the sanctuary. Yet I cannot emphasize too strongly that the experience of beauty is insufficient reason for a change of religion, for all these aesthetically valuable things disappear entirely when the Church is driven into the catacombs and made a spectacle to the world. Anyone who has no other reason than psalmody, vestments and incense will be unable to withstand the storm of total temptation.

I doubt whether I told myself these thing in my youth, but I do know that in this period of my life I did not lack an intelligent clearness of mind, but apart from the Eastern Church, the fate of which touched us little at that time, there was no other Church "under the Cross." In any case, the experience of this service, however much it impressed me, did not stir me to go in search of further and greater experiences of beauty in genuinely Catholic circles; rather it expressed itself in the desire that these values should be regained for the Protestant Church.

At first I was led by nothing more than a certain feeling for what befits a Church. I did not fail to reflect also upon the theology of the nature of the Church. Not the least of the merits of the High Churchmen has been the restoration to the German Protestant community of the notion that Christ lives on in the offices of the Church and in the seven sacraments. They have caused people to recognize this as one of the essentially valuable properties of the Christian faith. The unity and catholicity of the Church was understood in the sense of the Branch Theory, as a result of many contacts with the Church of England and with Lutheranism outside of Germany. Heiler's influence was especially strong in this. According to this Branch Theory, the unity of Christ's Church consists in the historic splitting of the original single Church into five great branches: the Roman, the Greek, the Lutheran, the Calvinistic, and the Anglican Churches. All groups possess partial truths and the unity of the Church is shown in the sum of their historically developed differences. It is true I did not feel very happy about this, for I could find no proof in revelation for any basic divergence or the right finally to split up. I could not see how the mutually opposed confessions were going to fulfill the prayer *ut omnes unum*. The World Conference of Churches at Lausanne in 1937, which I attended as an observer, caused me to see the critical situation of German theology; but, in the person of

Brent, the Anglican bishop of Buffalo, it elicited from me an esteem which made me hope that eventually an *Una Sancta* might be built upon a compromise of many minor points.

Even if the demand for symbolism were satisfied to some extent in the liturgical movement, and the concept of the unity of Christ's Church were realized to some extent in ecumenical work, there was another anxiety which could not be ignored, and with which I made contact immediately upon beginning my practical ministry in the Protestant provincial Church. A frightening disorder confronted me; it lay like mildew upon every branch of Church life, many-layered and deep-seated. And each time one looked, the diagnosis was much more shocking than the external symptoms led one to expect. The confusion in many parish registries, which I had to inspect as an ecclesiastical archivist, might have resulted from the technical inefficiency of the incumbent. But if I glanced into sacristies, which looked more like untended storerooms for secular objects than places in which to prepare for the sacred office, the roots of the general disorder were laid bare, even to the gaze of an observer like myself, who had only grasped the nature of the Church in outline. This parallels the attempt to "dechurch" the layman's life. The disorder which is to be found there emphasizes still more the fact that the layman wants to make use of the Church only on the special occasions of his life without being troubled by it at others; he simply wants the clergy to provide the religious trappings for an irreligious life. The "Regulations for Church Life" as drawn up by the provincial Churches are quite useless, the more so because these regulations are so loosely expressed that they lose all their force.

It is necessary to go deeper. The question is: What is the Church? Is it really a matter of grasping clearly and resolutely the contrast of an earthly fellowship of believers and a supernatural body concerned with salvation? The answer is no. The second includes the first. If the problem is rejected on the grounds that earthly things can never wear a supernatural garment, expressions which describe the Church as the Body of Christ and speak of her as our spiritual mother are devoid of sense.

The manifestations of Protestant Church life at synods, the undignified struggles of which I knew enough by hearsay (struggles over passing of Church laws and over ecclesiastical elections), closed in painfully upon me at the Kreis Synod and even in my own parish. It produced a distressing amount of opposition in premature and irrelevant application; and the efforts of men who might have been genuine church leaders were leveled down to produce the tiresome and demoralizing mediocrity of parliamentary procedure. Since no respect was shown for the spiritual office, the person of the clergyman became merely bourgeois. The office was stripped of any supernatural value, and the bourgeois way of life emphasized still more this process in which I, like the rest of you, was involved. I felt degraded, not in my personal attitude toward God and the community, but in respect to the office that had been committed to me, which was dedicated to the glory of God and the protection of souls. I learned this fact painfully because of the obstacles to my ministerial work which arose from these circumstances.

It was not surprising that I found no help from among my clerical colleagues of that time. I was not even understood. People shrugged their shoulders resignedly. The disorder was explained as a sign of life. Incursions into the study of theology were made fairly freely, but without for one moment thinking of the mission and object of the Church. We were like ships without a compass on a shoreless sea. So it was at least until World War II began. Nowhere did I feel more lonely than at the conventions. I felt like a child that had lost its mother and was experiencing a bitter sense of desolation and lack of security. I asked: Is there a home anywhere in this age in which we are perpetual travelers? Where shall I turn? The later Stoics had already failed by retreating pessimistically into subjectivism. Had not German Idealism, which had supplied German Protestantism with so many well-meaning but dangerous and explosive forces, come to naught because it was vastly disillusioned at not finding within itself satisfaction, purpose, and peace? The day was to come when men shouted at the walls and brought them tumbling down, or else they themselves were broken on these walls. It is for this reason, the excess of subjectivism, that the twentieth century is so pregnant with catastrophe both for the individual and the world. In these days of existential uprooting and homelessness, it is more than ever the office of the Church to be the rock of salvation, supporting man and leading him to divine truth. It is part of the essential nature of man that the assurance of being safe for time and eternity must be conveyed to him from the strength of objective validity.

By the manner in which the Protestant provincial Church exists today, this assurance is no longer conveyed. The room is empty; it lacks the venerable patina of age and makes no significant claim to be the bearer of eternal values. It is true that those who inhabit this room are not lacking in urgent seriousness, because there is still a sense of vocation and authority from above. However, the court in which ultimately valid decisions are made is no Church and no teaching office; it is simply the personal, subjective experience of salvation. In this subjectivity every objective result attained is liable to be dashed to pieces; it has no certainty of lasting; it is a prey to the demons of fortune, chance, and transiency. Thus it comes about that even after four hundred years of Protestantism no continuity has been produced. One is always, everywhere, making a fresh beginning, and this is typical also of the Evangelical Church. This evidence made me listen inwardly as I became conscious of it.

Some external cause led me one day into a Catholic Church in a suburb of southwest Berlin. The building was neither richly adorned, nor old, nor architecturally striking. Like most of the churches built soon after the turn of the century, it was characterized by a striving toward something which was only half attained. My eyes were offered no particularly striking liturgical service; it was a late afternoon devotion for the children making their first Communion. And yet, although no external picture provided the stimulation, there was suddenly, in its complex greatness and fullness, that ineffable atmosphere around me, the absence of which in Protestant churches had given me so many solitary hours. Here was order, authority, assurance of victory, reverence, and home. I had long known, as one knows things from books without really grasping them, that the Catholic Church has the power of sheltering a man lovingly in her bosom, as a mother does. Now I had experienced it for myself.

Yet I was far from allowing myself to be carried further on this wave. The sheltering motif, expressed in the liturgy by the words "Mother Church" and represented in art by the madonna of the sheltering mantle, is an essential part, like the aesthetic values, of Catholic fullness. In it the Church is following obediently in her Master's footsteps, for He told the inhabitants of Jerusalem that He would have gathered them as a hen gathers her chickens under her wings (Matt. 23:37). When as result of this experience, I was drawn again and again to the sheltering harbor of Catholicism, I was afraid that I was in the ranks of those who, tired of thought and broken by life's contradictions, seek rest and shelter "at any price." It is a sign of the serious spiritual disease of our time that the irrational, the zone lying in the underground of our soul, has become too powerful, that dreams and frenzy fill our consciousness instead of clear reason; and that the fear of the breakthrough of the imponderably-dark, paired with an odd love for chaos, causes us to rush into the arms of far-fetched speculation, come what may. Hence, the occult and theosophical sects, anthroposophy, and even political associations with a world outlook have today an increased importance; for many they have become closets in which they can hide their despair. I knew that I differed from these groups in belief, of course, but the same longing for shelter made me fear the reproach of the rational conscience. The Catholic Church was not going to be a mere "safe harbor" for me. And here, as in the case of aesthetic values, I demanded stronger reasons.

Added to this, there is the suspicion that the demand for shelter is an inverted desire for power, a suspicion which should not be readily rejected. This inversion could be a particularly strong motive for Protestant clergymen, for he comes from a distinctly subjective atmosphere. It would be worth something to enter a sphere in which there are things with objective validity and truths which cannot be whittled down, even if, in the new environment, one lacked esteem and sought none. The critical judgment with which I examined this, possibly only an accidental phenomenon of my experience, confirmed once more that the mere desire for certainty and an admiration for the imposing compactness of the Catholic Church were not adequate grounds for conversion. Anyone who decides to change his belief on grounds which are rationally so insecure makes a very questionable decision.

These experiences, confirmed repeatedly by feelings of homesickness in a cold world which forced solitude upon me, could have only a preparatory value, however loud their calls. If I understood God's purpose with a proper disposition of soul, they could only be an appeal, not the real summons leading to a decision. Then the war swallowed me up and regurgitated me again six years later. This period, which to untold numbers was a whirling waste or an abyss without inward recollection, proved to be a crucible of grace for me, and it opened up the decisive part of my way to the Catholic Church. On the day after All Souls', 1943, I was standing before the west front of the Rouen Cathedral. The setting sun of late autumn illumined the weathered stones while the modern buildings which bordered the square remained in the grey shadow of the November afternoon. Their soft glow only served to heighten the contrast. On the one hand, the longing for eternity, expressed in the Gothic dematerializing of the stone, was increased still more, while, on the other, the inexhaustible existence and grace of the Eternal became truly visible in one overwhelming picture. My eyes rose through the sculptures of the doorway arch right up to the highest little ornamental towers and *fleurons* above which soared the slender central spire like a bronze finger pointing heavenward. I tried to grasp in a single glance all the parts of the vast building, and to re-experience the thought of this mighty architectural projection in one enduring and impressive look. A "sober intoxication" came over me, a superrational clarity of mind, which made me fear to obscure what I had seen by putting it into words.

As I looked down at my grey-green uniform, the misery and poverty of our century passed palpably before my eyes and I asked myself, once more glancing devoutly at the pillars, arches, and traceries, what spiritual reality possessed the guild of masons when they undertook this work! And then it became clear. The most simple common denominator, that which unifies the otherworldly tendency of the upward-striving lines, the rigid distribution of the spaces, and the deep symbolism of the forms, is fullness itself. They knew something of the fullness that is God, of the fullness in which He reveals Himself, of the fullness with which He intends to remain with us until the end of the world. What I felt at that moment was no aesthetic intoxication, nor was it the intoxication of power, although the contemplation of a thing of beauty had initiated it. It was an ultimate, superrational insight into the connection between God and the world. The fullness of which I became aware was no fossilized mass with the dull seductiveness of the power urge; it was the fullness of order restrained in noble dimensions, a fullness that provides an urge to theologically rational understanding.

Allow me, dear brethren, to show you in outline, how the idea of fullness shines forth from biblical revelation, sometimes in words themselves and at other times, under the veil of different concepts. It will be but an outline, as I said, drawing the essential lines and making no claim to have traveled all the paths of cognition in this sphere. It results from the thoughts which accompanied my experience at the Cathedral of Rouen. Standing before it, I had grasped experientially the truth of the saying that the "Church is fullness," and subsequent reflection made me sure of it. As a result of the vision which this insight offered me, it behove me to examine Protestantism, an undertaking which did not seem to me too daring; for the concept of fullness is comprehensive and basic enough to arm one against any possible distortion of the perspective by malicious interpreters.

The question, then, is: How is the character of fullness exhibited in Christian revelation? What totality is meant when we speak of God's being and action, of His passage through the history of mankind, and of His exclusive revelation in Christ? What is the situation in Protestantism in regard to this fullness, in its purpose as a spiritual force, and in the form it assumes in the Evangelical Church? And I shall have to ask more particularly: Is the Evangelical Church fundamentally aware of her function as a bearer of supernatural truths? Does the Protestant understanding of religious universality correspond to the nature of the Church as the Body of Christ? Can the Evangelical Church distinguish between conformity with the world and aloofness in regard to the world, meanwhile harmonizing these concepts and giving precedence to the latter? Is the Protestant consciousness in a position to evaluate their tradition as the superior bearer of revelation in the sense of an unfolding of the truths of God, who is the Lord of all history and whose being is everlasting love? Does the Evangelical Church recognize a gradation of being which is not based upon purely worldly experience but upon an endowment both adapted to this world and serving the ends of salvation?

If all these questions could be answered with a facile "Yes" or "No," the decision would be easy. But the whole problem is exceedingly complex. There are no simple solutions. We often find the truth overgrown with weeds and at other times it seems to have been laid too bare. The fullness of spiritual life sometimes develop from poor soil, at other times it expires in the richest church. This complex situation is not to be found only in the Catholic Church, as is often emphasized; but also in the Protestant Church itself where it is gaining explosive force. It is a characteristic sign of the religious life. Hence it is that the answer is and must be, difficult to give.

My dear brethren, my next task, therefore, is to establish what the fundamental determinants of fullness are. In view of the recent literature of historical theology, I think I can take even your unanimity for granted on the thought that before Noah we find ourselves in the initial phases of God's historical revelations, and that the history of salvation, which is the history of a conviction that derives its hope and strength from the promise of Christ, begins with Abraham. "In you shall all nations of the earth be blessed" (Gen. 12:3). That is the fundamental charter of the promised kingdom of God. God utters it as the Lord of history, and the same God is the infinite fullness of being who is unfolded in this free act of grace. The words of God to Abraham contain, even at this stage, the five essential marks of fullness: 1, fulfillment in future time; 2, comprehensive unity; 3, election; 4, living transmission of the revelation; and, 5, knowledge of the laws of the metaphysical order.

Rational thought creates an image from the mathematical concept of spatial coordinates. In accordance with this, the horizontal represents the comprehensive unity; the vertical, tradition; the graduated division, order; the zero point (upon which God's perpendicular falls), His independence of space and time. These five essential marks which are neither accidental nor ingeniously artificial may be seen without difficulty throughout the history of salvation. The observational diagnosis is so vast that in this essay it can be sketched only in the most essential lines. Any discussion of fullness in the framework of the history of ideas will have to be set aside. Even if I limit myself to the Bible I shall be able to give only samples of my many findings. To give some order to the many questions arising, I shall use these five essential marks of fullness as my guide in the discussion; and at every point I shall ask, first, what the Bible has to say about it, and, second, how Protestantism stands in relation to it, and, finally, to what extent Protestantism neglects it in practice.

For the world of the Bible there is no secular salvation, no salvation apart from the superterrestrial God. The other-worldly origin of the revelation of salvation is the basic hypothesis for the self-consciousness of the nation of Israel and for its claim to leadership, just as it is for the Christian people of God. When the New Testament speaks of fullness, of *pleroma* (even in words derived from it) in the sense of a measure of value, it associates the pleroma-idea either with God or with Christ Himself, or with the concepts of time and fulfillment. "And of his fullness we have all received, grace for grace" (John 1:16). "For in him [Christ] dwells all the fullness of the Godhead bodily" (Col. 2:9). "But when the fullness of time came . . ." (Gal. 4:4). "The time is fulfilled, and the kingdom of God is at hand" (Mark 1:15). The concepts of fullness and fulfillment are extended (cf. Matt. 26:56; Luke 18:31; John 13:18, 19:28; Tim. 1:5; and Rom. 13:10). The association of revelation with time in the pleroma-idea is not accidental, for it means nothing less than that God's loving-kindness is made known in definite historical events; and in these, knowledge has its complete pleroma for man in the Embodied Spirit who alone makes history.

Jesus pours His own fullness of being into the prepentacostal company of His disciples (John 16:12-13); He extends this fullness to all time by giving to the Church eternal duration (Matt. 16:18); and as the greatest proof of His being filled with the logos, He communicates to the Church catholicity in space and time. "Behold I am with you all days, even unto the consummation of the world" (Matt. 28:20). In all the strata of life, in the little space of the individual soul and in the great space of history, the pleroma-idea is linked with the other world and gains its fullness from the abundance of the eternal God. The well-known words of St. Peter breathe this otherworldly fullness. They denominate Christians as "a chosen race, a royal priesthood, a holy nation, a purchased people" (1 Pet. 2:9). But the otherworldly connections of the people of God appear most clearly in the pleroma-idea in the following testimony of St. Paul. "And all things he made subject under his feet, and him he gave as head over all the Church, which indeed is his body, the completion [*pleroma*] of him who fills all with all" (Eph. 1:22-23). It is in this fundamental attitude that the superiority of Christianity lies; here that it rises above any seizure of world power by way of the idea of the "eternal return" such as is to be seen in antiquity in Horus, Dionysius, and Mithra, and in modern times, in the philosophical biologism of Nietzsche, in Ludwig Klages and, finally, in the mythologizing of race in National Socialism. In the rejection of these spiritual attitudes there is a clear unanimity among these confessions; the problem consists rather in the question as to what extent Protestantism can represent what is permanent in the flood of events and be for men a stronghold in a whirlpool of change. As we shall see, this question is of greater importance than it appears at first glance.

The Reformation concept of the Church found its classical expression in Article VII of the Augsburg Confession of 1530: *Est autem ecclesia congregatio sanctorum, in qua evangelium recte docetur et recte administrantur sacramenta* ("For the Church is the congregation of the saints in which the Gospel is rightly taught and the sacraments rightly administered"). At first glance and to the uncritical observer it looks as though everything is in order. It does not say, of course, who is the valid judge of the "right" teaching and who is to judge the "rightness" of the administration of the sacraments, but, for all that, the "saints" are considered to be superior to the world, and Word and sacrament are probably thought of as objective. But anyone who gives it close attention will recognize that the difficult point in the quotation lies in the word *congregatio,* a concept which expresses the fellowship of a flock, and if we hear further that Luther in the Great Catechism equates the *congregatio* with *communio* and *ecclesia,* the fundamental chord of the Reformers' conception of the Church begins to sound.

According to this, the Church, as far as it is an association of visible persons, has the character of a secular fellowship; its nature, however, consists in an invisible spiritual community, because, of course, its Head, who is in heaven, is also hidden. We all know today that the doctrine of an invisible Church is a theological dilemma which is not realistic with regard to the existential association of body and spirit. The problems raised by this teaching have been repeatedly discussed in the Evangelical writings of the period following World War I, and they come to a head in the question: How does the Word of God take on form in the visible association of Christians? If we examine the theological tenets of Evangelical Christianity, this question receives a positive answer among those who are interested in a Lutheran renaissance and among the liturgists, but among the spokesmen of dialectical theology, the answer is almost negative. But the answer of the first two groups who have labored hard and valiantly on behalf of the idea of the Church as the body of Christ, is not completely affirmative. The idea of the incorporation of Christians in the Body of Christ is understood by them as a future event, one which, at best, will occur at the end of time. In this idea of the Mystical Body the essential spiritualism of this invisible Church is not lost; rather it is enriched by the concept of organism. If one considers the previous pietism of the Evangelical Church, which was thoroughly subjectivist, it is something great to have learned that the Church of Christ is not a piling up of individual souls but a superpersonal creation of which the individual forms a part, like the member of a body.

But until this experience penetrates total corporeal and spiritual reality in space and time, it will remain, to those who do not accept it, a mere playing with views which are in themselves correct; and so long as the Word of God which is to take shape remains tied to the words of Scripture alone, in the sense of the principle of *sola scriptura,* the Body of Christ will have to dispense with the fullness of sacramental life, the breath by which the Church really lives. The sacrament of baptism alone remains to some extent intact. Among the deficiencies referred to, the need for the sacrament of the Eucharist is one which is still felt not only in parish practice but also theologically. In the Evangelical Church, the Lord's Supper is an objective element which requires fullness; but it exists within a subjectivist basic attitude that rejects fullness. The same dilemma is also to be seen in the current argument about private confession. The power of absolving from sin is still a matter for speculation. The idea that the Church is the appointed "storehouse" of grace is not adequately supported by the Lutheran notion that the Body of Christ is almost exclusively spiritual. The lines connecting the two ideas are few and too thin, and they break under the load which the problem places upon them. The chief cause of this deficiency, as I have said before, is the lack of the pleroma-idea in the Reformers' thinking, right from the outset. Is it not significant that Melancthon, even as early as in the Augsburg Confession renders the Pauline concept of fullness by *tota congregatio* (the whole assembly)? Instead of a concept which is filled with the breath of eternity, this concept is purely earthbound.

The practice of the Evangelical Church is in line with these suppositions. In hymns and prayers the image of the shepherd and the sheep, of pastor and pasture is constantly varied. Then upon this background the metaphor of the Head and its members, the idea of organism, is painted, but in such a way that the vertical gradation of the ecclesiastical orders is lost before the dominating force of the horizontal breadth of the flock. One looks in vain for the idea of fullness. Even in the ideas of the ecumenical movement the associative impulse is predominant. In the evangelical ecumenical movement, people are not concerned with the all-encompassing unity of the Mystical Body, which is the hallmark of fullness but with the fact that we are all somehow "brothers in Christ."

We observe the same process of covering up the idea of organism with this concept of the flock by the practical utilization of the space in the churches. Where Protestants took over medieval churches, the pews were moved right up into the space around the altar and into the most retired corners. It is not unusual for the altar to have been entirely removed from the sanctuary and placed in the midst of the congregation. That the designers of Protestant churches bore these intentions in mind right from the beginning is obvious from their preference for the circular construction and for galleries ranged in tiers. There is nowhere a place that is set aside to be a heavenward gesture to God, nowhere a "holy place." There is everywhere a stern seriousness which can be lightened only momentarily out of the shadows of concern with this world by such things as the strains of Bach. The space in a Protestant church is arranged primarily for preaching; the singing of the choir alone gives it a certain consecration. But when the congregation is absent, the place has no sacredness whatsoever; it is a mere place like countless others. This fact alone, apart from the absence of the Real Presence, renders useless the efforts made to keep Evangelical churches open outside of service time. What is one to do in a place, the symbolic character and power of which differs in no way from that of other buildings? This impression of an absence of sacredness is strengthened still more by the motif of creaturely fear which is expressed in the dominant concept of the flock, the *congregatio*. The close familiarity, reaching to the steps of the altar itself, the filling of every empty space with things of profane utility, the elimination of the silence by constant talking, hymn-singing and organ-playing—are not these all expressions of an existential fear? I have been inwardly oppressed over and over again by the fact that these buildings, even when seriously solemn, and even when pointing to the cross as the pledge of salvation, do not raise the mind but hold it down amid the things of earth. They are not capable, therefore, of sheltering the insecure and uprooted man of today and providing him with a home in time and space.

This lack of constructive force did not remain unnoticed in German Protestantism of the period following World War I. A demand arose for a material, a "tangible" holiness, for that strength that inheres in symbols. The liturgical revival, which came first from the *Berneuchenern* and the High Churchmen, is a symptom of this awareness of decline. Both groups, together with the ecumenical movement, have contributed greatly to the fertility of German Protestantism in the last three decades. They have opposed the exaggeration of the gap between God and man which seems inherent in the dialectical theology and have served as prime movers toward the working out of Protestantism's inner destiny. Because of them, German Protestantism was awakened to the ideas of the universality of the Church and its wholeness in the Mystical Body. But this departure and the attempt deriving from it to restore the fullness of the Church were accompanied by tragedy. The fissiparous tendencies inherent in Protestantism from its beginnings fell like a blight upon the groups I have mentioned. They could not agree; the different sorts of theological training they had received prevented them from really getting together to form an effective union. The *Berneuchenern* were faced with the fact that the Reformation experience, with its concern for the individual soul, was opposed to the mind of the Church and to the desire for form. The valid forms of expression of Church association available to Luther and his successors up to late in the eighteenth century were relics of the pre-Reformation period which succumbed to the process of disintegration. The High Churchmen did not get far because they could not heal the rift between their universal principles and their program of action which they desired to carry out within the framework of the provincial Churches, but could not effect because of the obstacles presented by this framework. It is true they had a priesthood which was in the Apostolic Succession, but they made no effort to become a part of the texture of the provincial Churches, for they lacked organizers and ecclesiastical leaders. Instead everything was dissipated in talk at their conferences and the harmony among them was forfeited. The movements grew old without bearing fruit, and the reality of Protestantism as an association concerned mainly with subjective ideas remained unchanged. The conclusion I drew from this was that no answer was to be found here to the problem of the Church's fullness.

God's first pronouncement in sacred history, the one to Abraham, contained the commission that he would be the center of fulfillment for world history. The people of Israel were aware that in this service it was "a blessing in the midst of the land" (Is. 19: 23). Jerusalem is called "the gates of the people" (Ezech. 23: 2). According to history, the communities of proselytes gathered round the synagogues in North Africa, Asia Minor, Greece, and Italy; communities recognized that universal monotheism had a value greater than that of their national cults; they had learned through the witness of the Old Testament that only in the belief in the

God of Abraham did they share in the fullness which is God Himself. It is from these groups that there came the minister of the Ethiopian queen (Acts 8: 26-40), the Roman centurion, Cornelius (Acts 10), and those proselytes of the civilized world of that time who were present on the day of the Church's foundation (Acts 2: 9-11). The historical expression of this pleroma is the religious universality of Judaism, which, unconditioned by myth and nature, but founded in morality and grace, gathers together the nations in the peace which rests upon such precious foundations (Isai. 2: 2-4). Strangers become the friends of God (Isai. 14: 1-2).

God's all-embracing love in Christ completes this spiritual building with His life, His sacrifice, and the institution of His Church. In the claim He makes, pleroma and *telos,* fullness and end, swing together in harmony like two bells: fullness, in His showing Himself equal with God, and end, in His sharing of His revelation through grace. We see the same harmony in connection with the approaching kingdom of God in the Church. It is an end which never ceases to be an end, and at the same time a fullness which is ever at the end. The Redemption embraces all of history and through the unity of the Church includes all the different nations and social groups (1 Cor. 7: 20-24; Gal. 3: 28). It embraces the ages, too, for the redeemed community is not a group of fanatics, but people living from the measure of fullness, and it knows that it is a community of people of the future in an age sick unto death (2 Pet. 3: 13; Apoc. 21: 3; *Didache* 10. 5). Every separate community is a reflection of the total Body of Christ. This is the keynote of the epistles to the Ephesians and Colossians in regard to the authoritative Christological pronouncements in the Gospels. God, Christ, and the Church are embraced in the pleroma idea. The signs of equality which we place between them are a "great mystery" (Eph. 5: 32); but in that very fact lies the deepest foundation of catholicity.

What then is the real situation regarding the claim for universal Christianity in the Evangelical Church? Let us first deal with this question historically. At the beginning of the Reformation, in spite of the interference of temporal rulers, the consciousness of belonging to the world Church, and of representing it in its own way, remained alive. On the whole, the traditional forms of church life persisted, and the discussion of Luther's experience of grace at first even heightened the consciousness of being the true Church and the means of fulfillment. The Reformation itself was at first conceived in terms of the whole world and the whole Church.

This attitude began to change when certain aspects of the different confessions grew more rigid. The system of provincial Churches grew up, and the Evangelical states declined to send representatives to the Council of Trent. In the Protestant realms religious thought was overlaid by the element of the absolutism of the petty states. The fact, for example, that a man who was parson in the Duchy of Coburg could also be a member of the consistorial court of the Electorate of Brandenburg, made the consciousness of the universality of the Church almost nonexistent, despite the fact that many of the old Protestant theologians did hold firm to the universality of Salvation. People no longer knew that it is part of the nature of the Church to represent, even in the most limited circumstances, the whole Church upon earth as well as the Church triumphant in heaven. The erroneous notion spread that the Church had begun as sects that developed from the teaching of the twelve Apostles, and had gradually worked itself up into the universal Church. People no longer grasped the idea that the Church has always been the Church by its very nature, and is such even in the "little flock" of the persecuted, provided it preserves the elements of fullness intact, which is its sacred responsibility. There was no longer any thought of an all-embracing unifying reality either in the horizontal plane of historic immediacy or in the vertical plane of future reality. People became isolated and thus the way was opened to more and more division. It is true that one was aware of other Christians beyond the pale, but how questionable their beliefs were! In practice the kingdom of God of the Evangelical provincial Churches ended at the customs barriers, with the last Prussian eagle and the last Saxon garland of rue.

Hence it came about that Christians, suffering under these limitations, left the provincial Churches in considerable numbers to join groups of revivalists and missionary sects. It is an undeniable fact that the religious life pulsated more strongly in these associations outside the Church than in the provincial Churches themselves. A marked tendency toward fullness was to be found in them, and their organizations acquired a world-wide extension long before there was any ecumenical movement. They liked to designate themselves with Old Testament names such as Bethel, Salem, Zion, Bethesda, Sarepta, Ebenezer, and Ezra. Of course, they could not tie up the ends of the chain of prophecy from those ancient times to the present day, but they certainly had in mind, by using these names, the supranational scope of revelation. Meanwhile, the German provincial Churches were building Kaiser Wilhelm memorial churches and Ernst-Moritz-Arndt churches. The feeling that such names were unsuitable for churches became so slight that almost a generation was to elapse before the responsible authorities thought of abolishing these and similar manifestations of state-church abuses. This did not happen until long after the disappearance of the ordinances of the provincial rulers, and only when, after 1945, the death of the "State gods" was experienced by the nation. At this point someone might object that we owe a great debt of gratitude to the Hohenzollerns and the Wettins. Did they then do any more than is fitting for a Christian prince to do? After all they only continued the foundation of churches and church institutions, a practice which had been regarded since the Carolingians as the obvious duty of an earthly ruler vis-à-vis the kingdom of God. And the fact that they were able to do this because of the vast wealth confiscated from the Church during the Reformation gives their solicitude a rather bitter taste. The greatest error of Protestant ecclesiastical principles does not consist in the state protection of the Church, in itself, but in the perverse order which set the throne above the altar.

When the ecumenical movement began to knock at the doors of German Protestantism, its adherents were still a long way from the thought of destroying these narrow regional growths. They were, therefore, only halfhearted about it, and they even attended world ecumenical conferences, declaring themselves, to some extent, opponents of a universal Church. In using the words "hesitant Germany" when speaking on the occasion of the death of Brent, the Anglican bishop of Buffalo, Adolf Deissmann, was not only uttering a legitimate German criticism of the inadequacy of the shortened basic creed, but was also expressing a general lack of enthusiasm in German Protestantism for the whole idea of ecumenism. I myself heard the Lutheran, Elert, declare in Lausanne in 1927, "We need the witness of the whole Church as a corrective"; such a statement as this indicates the limitation of the provincial or national Church. From the point of view of actual occurrences, it might be said that the individual Churches developed as a "corrective" to the world Church.

In three further observations, I should like to demonstrate the effect of this kind of half-love for the whole world-embracing Body of Christ:

1. I was deeply touched when I found out how earnestly and how loyally Catholics prayed for the reunion of Christendom in the prayers which are appointed for the season of Epiphany each year. I discovered that prayer for the unity of the Church is a constantly recurring theme, not only in the Canon of the Mass and the novena preceding Pentecost but also throughout the whole treasury of the Church's prayers. Outside of the Catholic Church the response to the summons to this week of prayer is often very feeble. Among Evangelical-Church people interest is very slight. And yet the suggestion for such a union in prayer emanated from a non-Catholic source. The appreciation of the whole meaning of the prayer of our Lord "that all may be one" is very lim-

ited among German Protestants. Ask yourselves, my brethren, to what extent, if at all, you take part in the annual Church Unity Octave.

2. On the Evangelical side the work of *Una Sancta* is done by men popularly looked upon as theological outsiders —but with what justification? In them the longing for a united Church has become a burning passion, but their number is small compared with the great mass of those who are not interested in these problems of the fullness of the Body of Christ. And the men who lead the Church and sit in key positions are silent. But even if an Evangelical provincial bishop were to join the *Una Sancta* movement, he could only do so on his own authority, for who could authorize him and to what purpose? These questions point up the difficult barriers that exist between the different confessions.

3. When, after 1945, the inhabitants of what were formerly good church districts were expelled from East Prussia and Silesia, it was expected in Evangelical circles that these immigrants would bring new life to areas which had become estranged from the Church. But the religious apathy of the population of Central Germany on both sides of the frontier between the zones has drained the considerable religious fervor of the Evangelical East. German Protestantism, then, has been unable to stand the test of the massive uprooting of its adherents from areas in which it had the upper hand. And this again is the result of the division into provincial Churches. Once these people were torn from the natural reserve of their native country, the land of their hosts could give them no religious home, and they failed even to find a house the spirit of which, wherever it stood,

could claim to be that of their Father's house; they lacked a consciousness that they were receiving this spirit.

Wherever I looked, I found efforts to develop a universal conception of the nature of the Church, i.e., its catholicity, checked by thinking on merely provincial-Church lines, or by an absence of thinking altogether. Nowhere in the confines of the Evangelical Church is universality taking on a visible and joyful form as the mark of the fullness of Christ's Body, nowhere is it becoming a general reality toward which all should strive.

The promise of salvation made to Abraham stands under the sign of God's choice and self-renunciation. The choice of Israel before all the nations of the earth comes about because "the Lord loved you and because of his fidelity to the oath he had sworn to your fathers" (Deut. 7: 8). Within the limits of the divine decree we are shown the love and the fullness of the divine Being. This motif is repeated in the New Testament. The poverty in which our Lord lived contrasts strangely with the majesty with which He faced up to the rich and powerful of His time. The same thing happens when apostles and evangelists, bishops and priests, majestic in the fullness of the grace they have experienced, stand before the judgment seats of the mighty of this world and confess Christ, the eternal fullness. What is the meaning of this contrast? By the history of Abraham and his seed, physical and spiritual, God teaches us that profane history is not to set itself up as absolute, as is the case in historical materialism. He also shows us that the naïve equating of sacred history and world history, such as we see it in the myths of pagan antiquity, or the cultural equating of these two historical spheres, as we meet it in the philosophy of history proposed by Idealism, misses the point of the revelation of divine fullness. God, the lord of history, who in this sense keeps His distance, realizes His plan of salvation through the redeeming community of the Church.

The history of salvation is that portion of world history which has been extracted by God's saving will. The chosen people of this special portion are guilty, like all other men; there is the adulterous David, Peter the denier, and the Church forgetful of its position as a servant. The tensions which render this line of death visible have acquired tremendous force in the field of sacred history. The Church as the "true Israel," the "Ark of the Covenant," "the heir of the Promise" continues this separate history in a state of fulfillment. Even within her the Devil has at times wrought havoc; the Eastern Church going its own way, the papacy of the ninth century, and the Vatican of the Renaissance. But the shadows have such sharp outlines merely because, in the same realm, the light is of superterrestrial brightness; and therein lies fullness.

If fullness consisted in the widest possible dispersion of views common to all and offensive to none it would soon be all over with. It would be dissipated and lost; it would be stifled in the jungle of opinions. Fullness must have a place of its own where it can constantly draw new life and in which it learns both objectivity and harmony in relation to all things. Life does not lack parallels. Let us consider marriage. The attachment of man and woman acquires its greatest fullness not in the unregulated intercourse of the sexes found among the primitives, nor in the casual exchange of partners seen among our contemporaries, but in the strict limitations imposed by marriage. The man who is to share in the fullness of life is not he who is everywhere and nowhere at home, but he who has a country which separates him from the stranger and at the same time affords him the harmony of fulfillment. Thus the Church is the religious man's home in this world of time and the place from which bridges are built by means of sacramental graces to his eternal home.

So long as the Reformers in their confessional documents spoke of the "Holy Church," they expressed their belief that there was a part of the world in which salvation occurred in a special way. Of course, this was not emphasized very strongly because the question of personal salvation was in the foreground of their picture; but up to about 1750, even in the areas dominated by the Evangelical Church, the Church was regarded in practice as the place in which life for time and eternity was fulfilled. Then things changed. A lack of Church unity, long present, but concealed by the power of habit, became obvious during the Enlightenment, once caesaropapism had prepared the way for secularization by a series of measures which blurred the frontiers between Church and State. If, brethren, you examine the old registers of communicants of your parishes, you will see that the annual number of communicants fell off with increasing obviousness starting with the second half of the eighteenth century. From that time on the Church is no longer the dominating architectural symbol but has to share is importance with the palace, and in the nineteenth century it yields to the factory and the exhibition building. The Catholic

Church, too, weakened in her external power by the sectarian splits, was driven into retreat, especially in the industrial areas, without, of course, attenuating or altering the knowledge of her unique mission. On the Protestant side the religious values flowed out into the world leaving no reservoir, and there was no possible place of reflux in which they could be renewed.

The spiritual form was given to this situation by Hegel in his *Lectures on the Philosophy of History* in which he declared that the state, and he was thinking particularly of Prussia, was the "manifestation of religion in the circumstances of reality." "Religion and state are, from now on, in harmony for the task of both is the same. The genuine reconciliation of the world with religion is now at hand." What Hegel taught, liberal *Kulturprotestantismus* practiced. We all know how it developed. First there was decay and a false spiritualization of ecclesiastical goods, and then the church wars and the secularization of cultural affairs, followed by the pious curtailment of culture and also of individual existence. I am well aware that *Kulturprotestantismus* is now no longer a force, but the bitter taste of that critical past persists today in numerous negative manifestations of church life. Furthermore, the expression "Separation of Church and State" was sketched into this period picture. A herald of these strivings was the dismissal from the government in 1850 of the High Consistory as the central ecclesiastical authority of the Prussian monarchy. This can in no way be regarded as a reconquest of Church freedom; what really happened was that a new secular consciousness pushed the Church on to a sidetrack because people had no more use

for it. It could go. It was, of course, a separation, but a negative one; from it neither objectivity nor harmony could be
regained.

As a result of this loss of fullness it was often difficult
enough to rediscover the signs of the dignity of the "royal
priesthood" in the provincial Churches. The National Socialist persecution of all things Christian certainly produced
in certain individuals heroic attitudes of religious loyalty,
but it was unable to raise the general Protestant consciousness from its earthbound condition. Henceforth one is in a
risky position and even gets to like this unstable stance. The
natural desire for sanctuary from the world that found a
home in Zinzendorf's Brotherhood [1] is still perceptible, in
spite of serious impoverishment, in the small groups of revivalists; but in the provincial Churches it fades into an
ever-deepening impotence. Furthermore, with the loss of the
educated and working classes, the Evangelical Church lost
just those people who have the spiritual breadth or the pug-
nacious courage to sustain the balance between separateness
and harmony. The lower middle class has neither one nor
the other.

Yet the deepest cause of this loss is not sociological, but
lies in a shortening of the theological lines, i.e., in the handing over of life to the world of secular values. The authority
of the Decalogue was transferred to the Council House. This
worked well enough so long as the principles were Christian. Little by little the old way of life was dispensed with.

[1] The Zinzendorf Brotherhood, also called the Herrnhuters, is a Protestant community founded in the eighteenth century by Count Zinzendorf.
Daily reading of the Gospel, absolute love of Christ, and sincere Christian
activity are demanded of the members.

The surrender was so complete that the excessive pressure of the secular world split the empty vessel and seeped through the cracks into the Church itself. When theology became painfully aware of this (just think of Troeltsch's unsuccessful struggles to free the absolutes of Christianity from historical relativism!), it found in Karl Barth a master merely of the "vertical" distance, that between God and man. The question of the "horizontal" distance, the relationship of the sphere of salvation (the Church) to the world, remained untouched. Where this latter distance is lacking there is also no harmony.

Then there is the question of the Protestant love for simplicity. Let me explain myself on this subject. Alongside the high cultural standard of life in Protestant lands, the life of the Church ebbs away in a "modesty" which is often indigent. We find immense, even excessively luxuriant manifestations of life around some wealthy industrialist of the West, and nearby, we find his church, the "simplicity" of which is completely lacking in dignity. And in the individual we find a rich organization of the religious upward-tending interior of the soul and beside it a radicality which is either aware only of the foreignness of the world or is entirely immersed in it. The "simplicity" of this thinking is not rendered essentially richer by the fact that in modern Evangelical spirituality the individual soul has replaced the Christian community. The problem of maintenance of "distance" occupies Protestant thought to such an extent that the concept of harmony, which can only be understood properly as temporal reality intervening from a distance, is scarcely considered. This deficiency leads to the adoption of extreme attitudes to the world, such as that lazy industriousness which remains insensitive to genuine holiness, or the exaggerated sense of worthiness we find in the "converted" among revivalists. All this, of course, is aloofness or its opposite, but it certainly is not harmonious. Now I hear the objection that there are no harmonies in this world broken by sin, and that to seek them goes beyond our creaturely situation. Yes and no! The tension of this opposition is eliminated in the figure of the Redeemer. In the Church His redeeming rule continues its work by the power of the Holy Spirit. Just as in the Incarnation the body of Jesus was exposed to the disharmonies of this world, so, too, is His Body, the Church. But just as the Spirit transfigured this body before and, still more, after the Resurrection, so the Holy Spirit creates a visible place in the Church for her gifts of grace and her ordinances. Here the simultaneous affirmation and denial of the world can be experienced in the rhythm of a lasting and commanding apprehension of values, and the Faith makes it all plain. Human beings are delivered from their condition of existing merely for themselves and transformed into new beings in the radiance of the life of grace. The New Testament describes this process in the following words, "But we all, with faces unveiled, reflecting as in a mirror the glory of the Lord, are being transformed into his very image from glory to glory, as through the Spirit of the Lord" (2 Cor. 3: 18). St. John expressed with classic brevity, and with his partly-concealing, partly-revealing power and splendor, the whole inward content of the "apartness" of the sphere of salvation, "Behold the dwelling of God with men" (Apoc. 21: 3). For years I tried to find the reality meant here in the Evangelical Church. As I did not find it, I became conscious that this Church lacked that fullness which is the essence of the Church of Christ.

If God is fullness, He is fullness in time, too. An expression of this quality is "mediating continuity," that is, the way of Israel to Christ, the Mediator, as the chain of promise, which begins with Abraham and which represents Him. "I am the God of Abraham, Isaac and Jacob." In every member of this chain we recognize the connection that goes back to the "God of the Fathers," and that goes forward to the promises of the eternal Covenant. "I, Yahweh . . . bind myself by an eternal covenant. Such a race shall spring from them, as all the nations of the world shall acknowledge; none that sees them but shall know them for a people the Lord has blessed" (Isai. 61: 8-9). Even the "remnant" (Isai. 10: 20-21; 28: 5; Soph. 2: 9; Zach. 13: 8-9), from the rending ordeal between Egypt and Assur-Babylon will join again, link by link, to the chain which began with Abraham.

Are not the two genealogical trees of Jesus (Matt. 1: 1ff.; Luke 3: 23-38) intended to serve the idea of continuity? Thus from the well of Old Testament tradition the message of Jesus developed as the fulfillment of that tradition. Jesus was no fanatic who despised what had been handed down, in order to renew the religious life from some wild root, even if His opponents saw Him in that light when He uttered his sharp, "Amen I say to you." Rather He cleared the dust of ages from the precious jewelry of the chain of promise beginning with Abraham; He washed it in the "blood of the lamb," which He Himself was, and crowned it with the assurance that He would remain for ever with us as the exalted Lord. He did not wish to destroy what had grown since Abraham but to fulfill it and to accomplish the promise. Jesus reveals His consciousness of continuity more clearly than He could by mere words in the way He brings about the transition from the last Passover to the Sacrificial Meal of the new covenant. First He plunges deep into the religious tradition of Israel, into the lawgiving of the God of the Old Testament, and the yearning of this people for deliverance; then he makes appurtenances of the old meal the symbol bearers of the new one, in which the deliverance is accomplished. He does not repudiate what has been; He crowns it with a lasting validity. He not only invites us to a perpetual repetition of this mystery, but by His divine power He adds a new link to the sacred chain of revelation. "As the Father has sent me, I also send you" (John 20, 21). But the earthly and historic bearer of this tradition is no longer one particular nation but the Church of all nations under the power of the Holy Spirit. That this tradition does not break off with the Apostles but is handed on from generation to generation, results from the foregoing, because the Spirit is divine and, therefore, eternal Spirit, and "Jesus Christ is the same, yesterday and today, yes and forever" (Heb. 13: 8). The Church's tradition, of which the most distinguished part is the New Testament, is the fruit of the idea of the continuity of salvation. It is the expression of divine fullness in the dimension of time.

That return to Old Testament theocracy, which is to be seen in early Protestant dogmatic theology and in Evangelical collections of prayers and hymns, took the place of the consciousness of catholicity, which had been lost in the religious struggles of the sixteenth century. In their return to a past which could no longer take on organic form, the Reformers, in practice, shut their eyes to the claim of fullness to be achieved here and now. But when the kingdom of David did anachronistically take on form, this happened in the sects. In regard to fullness in time, that is to say, in the continuity of the sphere of salvation, Protestant thinkers show themselves far less ready to make up their minds than they were before the ecumenical movement started. Of course, the idea that God is the lord of history and Christ its fulfilling center is strongly stressed in the face of the "sublime absurdity" of modern historical despair; but what led to this center and what proceeded from it, are things seen as having force only in the illuminations of great religious personalities. At the same time the "vertical" distance, the God-man relationship, is very much in the foreground, and, furthermore, it is usually associated with an accent of protest. Thus the word, "Protestants," in the original meaning, signifies the prophets in opposition to the defection of the Jewish Nation from its former acceptance of the Promise, Jesus in opposition to the guardians of the religion of the Law, Paul opposed to the false self-confidence of men, Augustine in opposition to the spiritual life of late classical times, Francis of Assisi against a Church which had become worldly, and Luther and the Reformers in opposition to the Catholic world in general. We can compare their witness to a row of electric lamps shining in the darkness; we do not see the chain from which they hang nor the cable which supplies all alike with nourishment. Yet the chain is really there and the current flows smoothly through the ages, clear and visible to all; for its source is in eternal truth.

All nations are aware of the inheritance from their fore-fathers, the preservation of which is a sacred duty. They are familiar with the office of handing on the torch of life. What the Bible does for tradition in the religious sphere is a process which is exactly comparable. But by habit the Evangelical Churches are still full of reservations in respect to the first 1,500 years of Christianity (which they often conveniently overlook), and they are strongly adverse to making an affirmative appraisal of tradition in spheres where Calvinism has been dominant, and are, to say the least, mildly suspicious even in Lutheran circles. Instead of adopting the lines of tradition in obedience to the God revealed in the history of Israel and its Church and accepting the conclusion, Protestants, in both thought and action, often brusquely cut these lines, leaving them hanging helplessly in their shortened form. Are, then, the links which hold together the chain of the history of salvation so devoid of the Holy Spirit that their traditions are unworthy of any more attention than is accorded to specimens in a museum? Even before the concept of the fullness of the Church had dawned upon me, I observed with astonishment the odd mixture of audacity and helplessness with which Evangelical clergymen demolished or else allowed to decay what little tradition remained in their parishes. I am well aware that there are things not worthy of preservation, but my object here is to point to a mental attitude which no longer bears any living relationship to the nature of tradition as the Bible witnesses to it. To the Protestant the operation of the Holy Spirit is understood in the sense of a direct invasion of the small space of an individual human soul; the historical operation of the Spirit in depth is overlooked. It is characteristic of the situation of German Protestantism that nowhere on a broad front do those deep spiritual powers take successful root, of which the external signs are concealed under the patina of apostolic dignity and the promise of future continuity.

That the nature of tradition in Catholic thought is not based chiefly on the preservation of venerable liturgical forms, but on the living power of the Holy Spirit, is proved by the fact that the historicity of revelation is raised to the sacramental sphere, namely in confirmation and ordination, which are conferred by the bishop. The man, upon whose head the hands of the apostles have been laid in the chain of spiritual succession and authorization, symbolizes, by his office and the official acts he performs, tradition, the fullness of the Church in time.

As early as 1519, in Luther's conference with Eck, Protestantism had moved away from the idea that the Church, as the mistress of tradition, is the bearer of revelation. There was really no need of the attempt made by Luther in the following year to deny, as unscriptural, the claims that confirmation and ordination were sacraments. This was already done when, in the preceding year, Luther had retreated from the time-spanning, objective world of the Church founded upon the apostles into moment-bound and ephemeral subjectivity. Thereafter, the practice of the Lutheran provincial Churches developed a divided attitude. On the one hand, the Church authorities drew up forms of ordination in which orders were conferred by the laying-on of merely priestly hands, for the office of bishop was now vested in the prince. Of course, this amounted to a "trickle" which was not historically justified, but it was strong enough not to leave the office of Evangelical pastor without some blessing and power. On the other hand, the ordination was turned into a prayerful and solemn ratification of a candidate's suitableness for the post of minister. As a relic of the connection with the unseen world there went with this the motif of vocation, subjectively attentuated and willingly seen as prophetic. This dual aspect is characterized by a semiaffirmative to fullness in time and by a definite denial of it. This is by no means a healthy polarity, no genuine *coincidentia oppositorum;* it results from lack of clarity. From the stream of the centuries a few tributaries, at times mere stagnant waters, are permitted to flow through the territories of the Evangelical Church; then suddenly this supply is declared to be dangerous to faith, if not completely destructive to it, and the stream is blocked up. The land would dry up completely if the torrential rain of God's Word did not occasionally water its fields; but what a loss of souls occurs because the drought is not overcome! And how much does the "torrential rain" sweep away simply because there is no adequate strength to withstand its impact? Continuity has gone; one is for ever starting again, as if yesterday was the first Pentecost.

How far the Evangelical Church is still aware of the distance which separates her way of life from the real man and his average capabilities may be left an open question. What is certain is that the exaggeration of the prophetic element, at the expense of the others which serve to anchor man in his world, has always led to the formation of sects. A feeling for the rhythm of historical development is quite foreign to them. The sect has no past, wants no future, and offers itself in a thousand fortuitous forms. It is the exact opposite of what I have termed "fullness in time," the complete antithesis of any conception of a religious society. Everything in it which appears to be fullness, namely fullness of religious fervor or fullness of fellowship, is a deception; it is the tabernacle of a moment, which tomorrow may be swept away by the storm. Protestantism is responsible for having created the fertile soil for such formations. The roots of this responsibility lie much deeper than the guilt of the Catholic Church at the period of the Reformation; this guilt consisted in a moral decline in Church life and in the obscuring of certain elements of the faith, not in the nature of what was properly Catholic. The cause of the formation of sects, however, is rooted in the very structure of Protestantism, both in its subjectivism and in its denial of the powers of tradition. In the proportion that the Evangelical Church fails to declare that the Christ-life has continued its work, and how it does it, after the biblical period, as well as in it, her spiritual referents are likely to be variable. The doubts which arose when there was some possibility of the provincial bishops making a doctrinal decision in respect to the "demythologizers" have made this quality once again shockingly obvious. Had the episcopal office of the Evangelical Church been permeated with the sacramental grace that is the spiritual heritage of the centuries, how differently would things have been managed in regard to certainty in this matter! As it is, however, a nervous unrest has been produced in institutions of learning and in pulpits; in the parishes the feeling varies between firm confidence and painful tenseness, between narrow defiance and a desire for order and breadth.

In biblical revelation we are concerned with an ordered fullness. The essential constituents of the pleroma previously discussed, i.e., otherworldliness, universality, election, and tradition, already include the notion of order. But this appears also as a distinct phenomenon in the Church of the old and new covenants and applies a structure of metaphysically stratified values which have their final cause in the justice and love of God. For the people of the Old Testament God's heaven is neither empty nor dark, nor is it full of terror-inspiring silence because mere caprice reigns there; it is filled with multitudinous hosts of angels (Dan. 7: 10). In ordered ranks they glorify the Highest at His throne, but in His service they throw countless bridges over the chasm of the gradations of being to man who is at the highest stage in the terrestrial scale of values (Ps. 8:6). Jacob's dream of the angels on the ladder which ascends to heaven, from the top of which God shows him a vision of tradition and promise simultaneously (Gen. 28:12-15), is the experiential expression of the fullness of order of God's creatures. When Israel is filled with the consciousness that God has determined the frontiers of the nations according to the number of the children of Israel (Deut. 32:8), and when the sharing of the Gentiles in the salvation of God ensues in proper order, the idea gains currency that the steps of His throne reach down to the most humble. There was never any lack of images drawn from the political organizations of the nations.

With the belief in angels, the New Testament takes over

the belief in the hierarchy of beings, at the head of which stands the "Father of all things" (1 Cor. 8:6). From the words of Jesus in regard to revelation we find the same images as in the Old Testament, only these increasingly build up the idea that the whole cosmic order is comprised in Christ through whom "All things have been created" (Col. 1:16). What is even more apparent than in the Jewish community of salvation is the idea in the apostolic message that the Church is the "heir of the promise," the core of sacred history, that it is, in other words, the fullness of all history. This fullness means that the historically unique event of the life of Jesus, which is beyond history and eternally present, remains both concealed and revealed in the Church as the Body of Christ, until the last shadows fade in the pure vision of our Lord's return at the end of time. Until then the Church is, with her offices and ordinances, a foretaste and mirror of the world to come. In her knowledge of this dignity she trod the path through the centuries until even I, too, met her fullness before the Cathedral of Rouen.

Fullness would be nothing but an overwhelming mass if it had no gradations and steps, if it had no divisions. Only as an ordered fullness can the essential nature of the pleroma be understood. From what has been said above, it is obvious that this order is not simply posited from considerations of utility, but it is conceived of as belonging by its very nature to the metaphysical realm. Now what position does Protestant thought take up in regard to this?

At the Reformation the endeavor to take God and His revelation quite seriously produced the radical subjective formula of solitary, personal experience. I do not want to discuss here the well-known and complicated question of the justice and limitations of this formula, which immediately became a bone of contention; my only concern with it is to show that this radical spirit makes fullness seem heavy and solid or completely impossible. The true mean, in which the elements of order occur, is seldom achieved in Protestant circles. In the Protestant way of life, with all the features of inwardness it announces, walking with God is conditioned by so powerful an inward attitude of distance, that in the long run too great a demand is imposed upon the individual believer. Of course, even amid such hard requirements, it is possible to find a harmonious mean, a balance lacking contradictions, of God's immanence and transcendence, of unity in trinity. Wherever Protestantism began to form a Church this attempt was made. But since the time when the "hidden God" received sharper outlines for the first time in the apocalyptic awesomeness of the late Middle Ages, the atmosphere has been so heavily charged with tensions that the Evangelical community finds itself open to the recurrent temptation to bridge the gap to a distant God in a "sudden" spiritual experience, or by "God in the heart," or to yield to it in a neurotic expectation of the end of the world. This trend ends in the belief that God's face is empty and is turned away from the world. God is felt as an immeasurable, even an awful, massif, and is so remote from men that they come to imagine that He has somehow plunged into nothingness beyond the farthest reach of human thought.

All this may sound very hard, and it may be objected that the mighty praises of Evangelical hymnody and the Church's faithful witness to the Scriptures proclaim the triune God; the Father, the Son, and the Holy Spirit. I, too, am gratefully aware of the graces and blessings contained in these things. But it cannot be denied that those movements which preach the irrationality of God and the absolute gulf between God and man, from the enthusiasts to the dialecticians, draw a picture of God which lays greater stress on the imponderability of the Eternal, the "jealousy of Yahweh," than on His fatherly love and His mercy. In relation to man, God stands like a huge mountain which rises undivided from a landscape only moderately undulating.

The tenuous relationship of Protestantism to the fullness of order is brought even more clearly to light by that picture of man which is based on Luther's experience of grace. According to this, man's sin completely destroys his ability to cooperate in salvation. God does everything Himself out of pure, free grace in the work of Christ. If man is confident in the saving power of Christ's cross, his sin will not be charged to him, although he remains a sinner. In the promise of grace, man experiences every consolation that can be granted him. The most striking characteristic of the Protestant process of justification is the fact that every line, both from God and to God, is slashed through with sin-pessimism. Man has even perverted his likeness to God, which was his in the beginning, into the face of the Wicked One. Since sin has been in the world, the eternal and the temporal, the infinite and the finite, can only be seen in sharp contrast. The rejection of moral responsibility is ultimately demanded, "For any act of ours is in vain, even in the best life"; at the same time the rise of childlike confidence in a merciful judgment is required, but this cannot basically alter the fact of the rejection of responsibility. This simultaneous denial and affirmation, which is always thwarted by a fresh denial, this state of spiritual hovering, only maintained by the stimulus of definite religious convictions, this unresolved tension in the Protestant doctrine of justification, offers no foundation at all for a scale of values appropriate to an earthly but redeemed existence, a scale ascending heavenward by grace. For the terror inspired by a radical feeling of worthlessness in the sight of God flattens out any consciousness of value and creates in the community people who are only "altogether sinners." This is an inner process to which even unreceptive natures have been subject and which gained in breadth as a result of Luther's experience of justification and which received, in the rising provincial Churches, a recognition far superior to any religious documents. And so, since that time, the Evangelical community has been understood to be a group of sinners rather than of saints.

This odd and extravagant mixture of a feeling of serious unworthiness and a childlike happy assurance is inseparable from Protestant spirituality. And the leveling tendency which emanates from it, and from a picture of God which hides His remoteness, finds its most genuine expression in a praying community that is completely disorganized. Nowhere in it do lasting patterns of life operate; everywhere one finds fleeting structures which disappear into themselves. Their places of prayer remind one of a cave which is illuminated for brief moments by a ray of light from an inaccessible distance; and the bizarre paradox which it evokes is "We are nothing, grace is all." The Evangelical provincial Churches, too, have not been unaffected by this spirit. I am thinking of that subjective pathos found in prayer at the altar and in the pulpit. I am also thinking of the absence of a principle of order, by virtue of which the human being, both cleric and layman, is incorporated for his soul's salvation, in a practical manner and for the good of the community, in the Church as a member of Christ's Mystical Body. I am thinking of the tendency toward isolation, the tendency to go one's own way, even at the expense of the Church's authority. Immature behavior of this sort leads to the open flouting of church leadership and to the small, yet public and lasting, scandals which, in consequence of the overrating of individual freedom of action, either cannot be overcome at all or can only be overcome late in the day. As a result subjectivism gains ground and the consciousness of unworthiness becomes in reality the very opposite.

I know very well that this situation, with all its accompanying phenomena, such as disunion in the Church and the estrangement of the masses, has been a matter of serious concern for at least a generation. Nothing has changed. The spiritual heart-searching did not reach down to that reality which is recognized in the statement of faith of the Epistle to the Ephesians, "The Church . . . is . . . the completion of him who fills all with all." For this reason any measures taken by the Evangelical Church in regard to Church order either remain on the surface or fall short of their mark. They are seen to be inadequate when the question as to whether divorced persons should be married in church becomes in the end merely a matter of opinion; they go too far when the baptism of a child is dependent upon whether its parents have been married in a church; and their aim is awry when confirmation is conditional upon a checked attendance at church. This matter of confirmation is already bristling with problems. These and other practical mistakes could occur only because the formerly rich structures of the faith have been impoverished by the consciousness of a deep-rooted unworthiness, and leveled to a "simplicity" which is as naïve as it is problematic.

The many-sided character of Protestant life, from the revivalist sects to the imposing provincial Church, is a distressing picture of shattered religious structures. The smaller the group is and the more enthusiastic its life, the less this situation is appreciated. The sect has built around itself the protective wall of a fanatic loyalty to its tenets, and it lives on the delusion that its own partial knowledge of religion is the "one thing necessary." But the Evangelical provincial Church which, today more than ever, might of its nature be a Church, has her fullness questioned on account of the indisputable fact of the decay of her holy orders. This lack is felt to be very painful; the fundamental problems, so urgently discussed at present, have their origin here.

My dear brethren, I have asked Protestantism if it is satisfied with St. Paul's statement that the Church is fullness, not only in a general way, but also in the five ways in which fullness comes to fruition. Again and again I came across considerable inadequacy in respect to the fullness of revelation; but ever present has been a strong desire for all those values which have been brought to light from a buried heritage or glimpsed beyond the limits of the confessional hedge. The profound nature of the rejection of the elements comprised in the pleroma-idea is seen in the fact that the obstacles to fullness loom larger than any joyful restoration of the lost fullness.

In this connection some of you will have expected a discussion of the so-called "dividing doctrines." However instructive it might be to assess the position of the problem of free will, the meaning of the Sacrifice of the Mass, Mariology, and the nature of the papacy in relation to the pleroma-idea, I have deliberately avoided it for several reasons. In the first place, these theological points were not central in that basic experience I had before the Cathedral of Rouen. My acceptance of them was easy once I had realized the nature of fullness as a sign of divine revelation. Next, the "dividing doctrines," important though they are, do not seem to me adapted to render man as a whole accessible to what is essential in Catholicism. The problem of the relationship of grace and freedom often remains on a purely intellectual plane, and the shifting centers of gravity in its theological depths are not grasped in terms of existence. The fact that Christ's sacrifice in the Mass is regarded as continuing for all time takes for granted the belief that the Church is Christ's Living Body. Unfortunately, the affection shown to God's Mother is commonly understood only as a means of ventilating man's need for a mother; it is substituted for, according to taste, by such "profane" figures as the "Mona Lisa," "Queen Louise," or Feuerbach's "Iphigenie." Those who live in a Christendom that is torn asunder, envy and respect the unity given by the papacy, but they go no further. Finally, it is easy enough to find the "dividing doctrines" treated with great thoroughness in almost every book of controversial theology and apologetics.

I have been much more interested in throwing light on Protestant forms of living from the angle of fullness and judging from that angle the total picture they make. The lack of Christ's fullness, which oppressed me on all sides, drove me out of the Protestant camp. I felt like someone whose passport had expired and could not be renewed. What was I to do now? Three possibilities occurred to me: retreat, attack, or convert.

To retreat with my experience into my own inner world and to renounce the realization of what I had experienced would have been the simplest solution. The subjective tendencies of the Protestant way of life might even have included such an attitude, but the realities of my office reminded me daily of the need for inner decisiveness. Besides which, I was not "tired" enough to retire into a questionable state of pseudo-contemplation.

Was I to attack? As long as I was in close association with the High Church Movement I thought I had this vocation. In view of the fossilized greatness of the German Evangelical Church, it would have meant making a life sacrifice. My intelligence, however, told me that no previous reflections I had had in the Evangelical Church showed any basis for the achievement of a real goal. Such a goal was still far from being in sight, for many think that universal fullness can be attained solely with the help of a swarm of major and minor sects, with never so much as a glance at the Catholic Church. The necessary basis is lacking even among the Evangelical participants in the *Una Sancta* Movement; for I am unable to see that they are, by joint action, even able to deal with their own Church with the object of equipping it for the spirit of fullness.

My refusal of the Protestant way of life would not have involved an immediate acceptance of the Catholic Church had it not been for the fact that I felt I had exhausted every other possible way to reality. It was the Catholic Church which had stood at my side like a loving and patient mother in all my previous reflections. Not only had the first stirrings of my youthful longing for fullness been inspired by her; my very thoughts were directed upward by the noble structure of her spiritual cathedral, and they apprehended in her the nature of Christ's fullness.

Those Protestant theologians, who like to speak of man's situation as one of "daring," regard conversion as a breakdown in the face of the inevitable uncertainties of the world and as a flight into a false security. Did Christ promise salvation to poor mortals only to leave them uncertain of it? Did He not in fact make them whole? And after Pentecost did this healing become once more a mere promise? Does He not intend to stay with us until the end of the world? All who have "come home" spiritually will witness with me that they have experienced the Church, in her high motherly dignity, as the fairest sign of the love of their exalted Lord. They will agree that such a realization is the very truth, and that this religious *Lebensraum* is guaranteed by the Catholic Church insofar as historical continuity and wholeness of revelation are concerned.

Others object that conversion in our present historical situation is desertion; they say it is presumptuous to wish to anticipate by one's own actions God's plans to unite His Church. The problem of divine providence and human freedom of decision which lies behind this thesis is explained away by its defenders in an aura of passive quietism. This in itself is already dubious. But still more dubious is the assumption that the one, true Church is a gift of the future. If this were so, conversion is, of course, superfluous. In this case a man ought to remain in the Church of his fathers and serve the future unity of the Church in the framework of the possibilities given him. But what if the truth has been revealed to me, that the one Church of Jesus Christ has existed without interruption since the first Pentecost, and has assumed its maturest and most exalted form in the Catholic Church! May I then wait only at her gate and look longingly into her windows? In this situation am I not bound, if the Lord's call to me is so total, to enter the historically concrete area of this Church and to partake of her blessings as a living member? Is it not, then, a clear sign of a morbid religiosity to wish to remain outside, simply to experience in full the danger of uncertainty? My position has been determined by the fact that the spiritual experience of fullness, together with my consequent critical examination of the various Churches, caused me to realize that the lack of fullness in Protestantism is no mere superficial and transient phenomenon; it is rooted in its very nature and has a force all its own. On the other hand, I perceived that the Catholic Church, in spite of the weakness of many of her members, has assumed the "fullness of Christ" and is permeated completely by it, she lives on infallibly in the supernatural fullness of grace provided by her sacraments. However, in spite of this contrast between the two faiths, I do not look upon my conversion as a turning away from downright error. I shall not burn what I have previously adored, nor have I ever burned those things which I now worship. The saying to which I referred at the beginning of this account does not apply here. I have already said that solutions are not so easy and that they are often found with contrasting designs. I do not abandon the positive values of my past church life, nor do I regard myself as having moved into a new world completely opposed to the old. I tend rather to understand my step as one going as it were upward from a religious world which, measured against revelation, is incomplete, into a sphere in which the fullness of being, of grace, and of glory enfold me in perfect love. I have come through the gate to enter into the sanctuary, but with me I have taken all the spiritual luggage of my former wanderings, all our common Christian inheritance and any of the fruits of fullness which grew there.

I feel obliged to emphasize this last point for I have a fear and a feeling that this account will lay me open to the criticism that I am unprepared to see any traces of fullness in Protestantism. It is not so. The non-Catholic world does possess elements which vouch for the spirit of fullness, those elements from the pre-Reformation heritage which historical conditions allowed to remain. Even if they have not been nurtured they have nevertheless been kept, although at times, it is true, they were kept like pieces in a museum. Added to this is the fact that German Protestantism has sent its roots deep into the fullness of Evangelical hymnody, a special blessing of the Spirit. But the recognition of this truth does not remove the fact that the nature of Protestant emotion, determined as it is by religious radicalism and subjectivism, is averse to everything which stems from the true spirit of fullness, everything which includes supernatural order, historical fixity, maternal protection, disciplined breadth, and participation in the divine life.

The nature of Catholicism consists in the apprehension and affirmation of fullness. This is so central a part of the Catholic mean that all earthly forms of order are determined by it. In a word, thought consists of a thinking from fullness. Now if we do not always succeed in making this fullness conscious, this is because the whole of truth is not available in every point of our Christian history; and if developments sometimes lag behind the fullness perceived, the cause lies in the manifold limitations, geographic, climatic, social, and historical, which are imposed upon life in this world. We may take in the wholeness of the world with the eyes of faith. However, what is creaturely in us can never reflect more than a fragment of that total reality; a fragment, it is true, which by becoming visible renders the whole transparent. The difference between thought which is permeated by the faith and thought which is an attempt to master things without God lies in the fact that the elements of fullness are entrusted to the believer. These elements enable him to attain to a genuine transcendence, to a breadth which is not squandered in enthusiasms, to a detachment which does not lose its practical connection with the things of earth, to a historical sense which is not vitiated by relativism, and to a system of order which guarantees fullness.

The harmonious interaction of all the basic elements has

reached its maturest form in the Catholic Church. The word "and" is an expression of this synthesis. It is only a small conjunction, but it is of significant weight. One example of many from the New Testament is the greeting of the Epistle to the Philippians: "Paul and Timothy, servants of Jesus Christ, to all the saints in Jesus Christ that are at Philippi, with the bishops and deacons: grace be to you, and peace from God our Father, and from the Lord Jesus Christ." This "and" which is utilized four times is intended to make assertions concerning the elements of "fullness." "Bishops and deacons": the Church is, in the gradation of her offices, a living organism whose head is our Lord Himself. "Grace and peace": the life which is redeemed and the world which is "whole" come from God's hand, but He brings grace and peace only because we cooperate in giving shape to peace. "Paul and Timothy": teacher and scholar, bound by the chain of loyalty to the Master from above. "God, our Father, and the Lord Jesus Christ": a bridge over the abyss between the name of God and the name of the man Jesus, constructed from the wood of the Cross and the stone rolled away from the tomb; Jesus who was exalted to heaven by the royal title and in whom the Church on earth shares in the communion of saints.

The Church continued then to build in the spirit of this "and"; she unfolds her mystery in dual concepts such as grace and freedom, faith and reason, tradition and Scripture, unity and multiplicity, spirit and body. It is unnecessary to say what Catholic doctrines and thoughts lie behind these, because I should only say what is generally known and might even repeat myself, for much is implicit or has been clearly said already in my discussion here. There are only two more points I should like to raise. The Catholic "and," unlike the Protestant "alone," has never become a controversial formula. But then, and this is the most important point here, the "and" builds upon the great architecture of all life, as it is symbolized in the proportion and complexity of Gothic cathedrals. It builds, namely, upon the gradation of being that finally reaches to God, which is rhythmical and orderly and goes in an ever upward ascent; it builds likewise on the hieratic descent of heaven's blessing upon what is earthly.

*   *   *   *   *   *

From the beginning the Catholic Church has possessed as a gift of grace the divine commission of fullness, and has made it real in doctrine and in the ordering of life. The fullness of the triune God has been poured into the Catholic Church. From her we have received the fullness of the Word as it is contained in Holy Scripture and unfolded in tradition. In her is to be found the fullness of the sacraments with which she feeds us. She is organized in the fullness of her offices; she mirrors in the teaching, priestly, and pastoral offices, the threefold office of Christ. She is the fullness of the ages made evident in the rhythm of the liturgy of the church year. In her fullness is included the one Creed and the unanimous praise of every nation on earth.

The sixteenth century forced her into the struggle to preserve her essential principles, and this defensive attitude had a detrimental effect upon the happy development of her fullness. But since she never cast off that essential character permeated by fullness, it was given her, from about the middle of the last century, to rekindle one light of fullness after another. Through personalities such as Ketteler and Leo XIII, social questions have been clarified; theology has been stimulated by a renewed interest in the thought of St. Thomas; while new life has been inspired in the practical sphere by the liturgical movement and the apostolate of the laity. In regard to the desire for peace in society, acceptance of a spiritual leadership and, not least, reunion of Christendom, it is devoutly to be hoped that this development is far from ended. While the Catholic Church has seen many earthly organizations die, and many Christian sects disappear in the whirlpool of ungoverned opinion, she herself has been given the graces to survive the ages without aging; the grace of unity without uniformity, the grace of distinctness without withdrawal from the world, the grace of completion while continuing to develop—in short, the grace of fullness without becoming abandoned to a sacrilegious self-intoxication.

My dear brethren, it was not my intention to present you with a study of Protestant beliefs or an apology for Catholicism. What I wanted to do was to tell you how I was led. I am very conscious that the total picture, within and without, is much richer than I have been able to show here. I shall be quite pleased if I have succeeded, in the light of my experience, in making clear the things which separate and distinguish the creeds. In view of the weight of nontheological restraints, it is probably useless to expect more.

It is not without compunction that I have separated from you. After all, almost two decades of work together for Christ could not be insignificant to me. My decision is one of fundamental importance, a decision concerning our outlook on the world and the nature of God. It implies a close attention to eternal verities and an intelligent obedience to God's call, which I am following. I am taking this path alone as many another has done, yet I think my example may not be without some propaedeutic significance. Protestantism has let things go from their religious context into a secular solitude and, hence, bears a heavy responsibility for the religious and cultural heedlessness of our civilization. At the present time, in which people are painfully aware of this grave situation, Protestantism is no longer in a position to restore the orphaned children of its creation to their home in the order of revelation; it lacks the mother's protective hand and the father's sure direction. If today we were to be presented once more with a new *life-form* rooted in the transcendental· sphere, I know of no other institution capable of reuniting the things that have been scattered and transfiguring them for eternity than the Church in her Catholic form. And if I correctly understand the signs that are set in the present and coming decades, together with the increasing number of converts from the ranks of spiritual leaders, I cannot help but think that the regathering and reconstruction of mankind under the banner of Catholicism has already begun. And I thank God that I may say with feelings of gratitude that I was present at that time.

Please remember me in your prayers, my revered and beloved brethren, as I shall remember you.

HEINRICH SCHLIER

A Brief Apologia

I CAN TRUTHFULLY SAY that I did not make my own way into the Catholic Church, but I have taken that path. For me it was the given path, and because of this it was also the bidden path. I cannot explain this path, because I do not see it now as from a lofty stance, nor do I survey it as from a goal which has been reached. What I see, at the most, are a number of cul-de-sacs up which I have walked and to the ends of which I soon came. They were quite unconnected, but for all that, they did constitute *a* way. However, this way has only one goal, which is God. If I wanted to reconstruct it, I should say a lot that is unimportant and neglect much that is important, and, on the whole, I should never know if my picture was an impartial one.

Yet is it by no means necessary to describe my path into the Church. My intention here is not to satisfy pious curiosity, but simply to make the truth heard here as elsewhere. Much more urgent than a description of my way is a statement of what contributed to, and helped me to take, this path. Most important of all is the fact that I mention the reasons which impelled me to take this path. Since, in addition to this, I happen to have been a clergymen and a theologian outside the Church, although at heart I was already for quite a while within her, I owe an apologia on these grounds alone. I owe it to those whose company I had to leave and to the Church that accepted me.

I could mention a great many of those things which contributed to my entry into the Church. From the viewpoint of the deepest considerations, everything that occurred to me in life contributed a little, but what led me was often that which had no appearance at all of leading me in that direction. How otherwise can I possibly understand my years of apprenticeship in the school of my great teachers, Karl Barth, R. Bultmann, and M. Heidegger? I hope these men will allow me to mention them gratefully for, in the long run and in a hidden manner, they join cause with me. But I am not writing my life story. I shall mention only in passing a few circumstances, meetings, and experiences, lest anyone should get the impression that my reasons for conversion belonged only to the realm of the distantly abstract and were not part and parcel of my life, as indeed they were.

There is no doubt that the simple piety of my father, which bore the stamp of Bavarian Lutheranism, had an influence upon me of which I was unconscious. It had many "Catholic" features. Besides, I feel that my early life in Catholic surroundings was not without some influence. I grew up in the shadow of a tall church which was named *Zur Schönen Unserer Lieben Frauen* and our teacher at grade school explained that *zur Schönen* was equivalent to *zur Schönheit*. Hence the church was dedicated to the Beauty of Our Lady. At that time I often thought that it was an odd name for so vast, and by no means especially attractive, a church. It was a brick building in the Gothic style.

This town, in which the old university was still standing, within whose walls St. Peter Canisius had taught for a time, and its atmosphere, which was Catholic and at the same time tolerantly Catholic, preserved me at any rate from anti-Catholic bigotry. Right from the beginning, because of my native environment, I was disposed favorably toward Catholicism. Even as a convinced Lutheran I never felt any antipathy for the Catholic Church. On the contrary, she had a warm place in my heart. But, in retrospect, the influences of one's environment are not easy to appreciate or to explain. Those influences which were due to definite meetings with Catholics and the Catholic spirit are much more tangible and have a much greater effect upon one's consciousness. It is not my intention here to make any comparisons or to express any judgments. I have no right to do so. Nor, so far as I know, have I lived with the illusion that Catholics are not the same as other men. I have never been unaware that both wheat and chaff are to be found among them. And yet it did occur to me, and it was not so immaterial to me as it might seem to many others, that Catholics had something about them which did not quite fit into the general time scheme. This may be merely due to the fact that they have a strikingly compact belief. The fact also struck me that the Catholic is somehow more humble and devoted; for among them even the men kneel.[1]

I noticed, finally, that in his knowledge of himself and of sin in the concrete, the Catholic possesses a certain merciful breadth of view and kindliness, even if this is only due to the fact that he applies them to himself. It was just this quality, though in purer form and in greater depths of character, that I found in individual devout men and women. I am using no merely "edifying" language in calling this the "spirit of Christ." I, of course, would not name here any people of this sort who are still alive. But among the dead I remember one man, the Abbot Angelus of Ettal, a real witness of the Lord and a true son of St. Benedict.

[1] Among the various Lutheran groups, there are some in which men do not kneel when praying. [*Translator's note.*]

And I remember, too, the company of his sons, small in number at that time, who taught me the meaning of their rule: *omnes supervenientes hospites tamquam Christus suscipiantur.*

But I recall, too, a man of quite a different stamp, another genuine son of *his* spiritual father, who was imprisoned at that time in Ettal: Father Rupert Mayer. He seemed to me like a captive lion impatiently walking up and down behind the bars. How he waited day and night for the freedom to be of service! In the face of such, and many more, humble, ready, merciful, and resolute men, who followed Christ in community or alone, my Protestant dislike for the pattern, and for those who model themselves upon it, gradually retreated into the distance. What absolute absurdity to think that they contradicted the Word! In this connection, nothing makes a stronger impression than example, and there is no more intensive listening than imitation.

Of course, I met the Catholic spirit in Catholic literature, too. I will not deny that for years I frequently bought those little pamphlets which are seen in the back of churches and learned something from many of them. Truth takes on many forms, many of which are quite unassuming. Besides these the Catholic periodical *Hochland* early attracted my interest and clarified many problems. I believe I have read it regularly since 1927. Camus (*Wisdom of Francis de Sales*), Möhler, Newman, Theodor Häcker, Bernanos, Claudel, and the far too little known essays and treatises of Erik Peterson were the very varied "fishing hooks" of the Holy Spirit. I owe my dogmatic instruction above all to the work of Diekamp. Although at first this subject seemed dry and foreign to me, it gradually fascinated me as I got into it more deeply. I perceived that theology in a concrete sense took revelation for granted, and saw that even in this science everything has its place.

All that I have merely been able to hint at by quoting a few names would have been far from affecting me profoundly if my preparedness, or rather my longing for the "Catholic," had not been strengthened by distinct experiences. These were the ones I had in connection with my pastoral office and in the struggle of the Confessing Church. These discussions which lasted for thirty years represented the stand made by brave and devout men for the Christian basis of the Evangelical Church, in the face of that ecclesiastical political movement with religious trappings that culminated in the German Christians. It was a stand also against the anti-Christian Third Reich in an effort to regain the "Church" for the Evangelical Church.

Although I always wholeheartedly supported the resistance of the Confessing Church both to Hitler's Reich and to the opportunist enthusiasm of the German Christians encouraged by it, I was equally aware of the hopelessness of all efforts in support of the Church. This was borne in upon me in the administration of my parish and at the church synods. These efforts were rendered sterile because certain concrete principles were not accepted. It became more and more evident that there were not only different views as to the meanings of the confessional documents but, which was much worse, that these documents, which had once represented the foundations of the Evangelical Church, were no longer recognized as such. The most unfortunate thing of all was that the theological conviction, that a confessional document was, in its concrete content, a binding dogmatic basis of the Church, was rejected and vigorously decried as "confessionalism." The characteristic and false antithesis was that the affirmation in the sense of the confessional document was unimportant, but what was important was that one affirmed in the spirit of the confession itself. The creed contained in the sense of the confessional document was only a signpost directing one's faith along a certain road, for faith was not an assent to particular articles of belief (this certainly is not all it is) but something quite different. In this way, as I began to see more and more clearly, the dogmatic principle was replaced by the charismatic. But the personal spiritual gift of personal faith kindled by Holy Scripture rests upon dogma; it cannot step into its place. Charism may well be the activity of the Church but it is not her foundation.

Something similar came to light in the struggles of the Confessing Church when the subject of "office" and its institution was discussed. When I consider in retrospect on what authority I fulfilled my office, I am horrified. For, fundamentally, the authority I had, was derived only from my professional training, my own decision, the assent of the parish, and the recognition of some church leader or authority. In the Confessing Church the charismatic basis of the office gained the day. This, oddly enough, was combined with a sort of bureaucratic conception. I found the situation less and less satisfactory.

Today things have settled down again in the Evangelical Church and it looks as though people have become resigned in the face of these and other fundamental questions. In the silence which has descended, remarkable but quite important theological processes are at work. An ecclesiastical bureaucracy makes disciplinary decisions about dogma. And in theology many dispense with the so-called "formal principles of the Evangelical Church," and the canon of Holy Scripture; the latter being replaced by the canon of the coming of an inspiration, kindled by the words of Scripture. Side by side with this there is the recurrent attack upon the sacrament of baptism in the form of a theological and practical refusal of infant baptism. Added to this, there is the misunderstanding of the so-called "demythologizing" of the New Testament, which is involuntarily calculated to rid the faith of the Evangelical Church of any substance. Is it not natural that these and similar developments should make people look with increasing urgency toward the Catholic Church, which, after all, in spite of wounds and periodic setbacks, has preserved the fundamental principles, and has, therefore, remained the Church of Christ, eternally capable of renewing her life?

Circumstances, meetings, and experiences of this sort cooperated to make me Catholic in outlook, but the impulse which decided me came from another quarter. It came from the New Testament, the interpretation of which had become my profession. The New Testament gradually made me ask whether the original Lutheran creed, and the new Evangelical faith which deviates considerably from this latter, agree with its witness. Little by little, it convinced me that the Church it has in mind is the Roman Catholic Church. Thus my way to the Church was a truly Protestant one, if I may so express it. It is a way foreseen, although, of course, not expected, in the Lutheran confessional documents.

In this connection I must mention one other thing. It was the New Testament subjected to an impartial historical interpretation which led me to the Church. This does not contradict what I later affirmed when I said that any interpretation of Holy Scripture must be in the spirit of the Church, if it is to be a true interpretation. For the spirit of the Church includes also the impartiality of genuine historical research. And this is carried out, too, not in the spirit of slavery to fear, but of sonship. Historical research really objectively open to historical phenomena is also a means of illuminating truth. Thus it, too, can discover the Church and be a way to her. For this reason I am still grateful to those who introduced me to this work.

But exactly what was it that the New Testament revealed to me as, little by little, it rendered the Church and her faith more visible to me? Here, of course, I cannot answer this in detail with all my reasons. To do this I should have to write a detailed theology of the New Testament. It is only possible to indicate a few insights which I gained from the New Testament and which drove me decisively on to the road to the Church. The first, if I arrange my thoughts somewhat objectively, was this: The New Testament itself recognizes and propounds the historical fact of the unfolding and development of the apostolic deposit of faith which is so fundamental to the understanding of tradition in its wider sense. In the New Testament Christ's free giving of Himself through the Holy Spirit in the Church is in "principle" captured and documented; that is to say, we find its origin and beginning there. And it manifests itself in connection with the apostolic heritage, which cannot be contained only in the New Testament writings, more and more in the total tradition of the Church to this day. Otherwise, the development of the "Jesus tradition" apart from the gospels as well as within them cannot be theologically explicable. One can only understand it as the "self-exegesis" of the *Logos,* Jesus Christ Himself through the Holy Spirit through the faith of the Church. This is particularly obvious in the Fourth Gospel. The process of the development of the primal events can also be seen in the epistles of the Apostle Paul. To cite one example, this is not only visible in the development of his concept of the Church, but in the development of the actual historical phenomenon of the Church. In the pastoral letters, one is already faced with reflections upon the factual basis of a developing tradition, reflections induced by a new situation in the Church.

Thus no one can deny that the New Testament recognizes the process of development of both the historical phenomena in themselves and the understanding of them. Research in historical criticism has made us conscious of this fact. It is possible to interpret this development in many different ways. One may explain it as a logical evolution of the essential deposit, as a gradual discovery of what is implicit in it; or one may see it as an improper development, a development which amounts to a departure from, and even a contradiction of, the original facts. In this case it amounts to the acquisition of new matter, of accretions, and is, therefore, a deviation from the original words and events. In my opinion this interpretation of the phenomena is shortsighted, because it merely sees things on the surface, where they often clash, and not in depth, where they are in harmony; but it also amounts to adopting in the sphere of historical research the dogmatic judgment of the Reformers and pietists who claimed that the Church had apostatized. But it is food for thought that time itself has brought this argument *ad absurdum*. For, if the theses of the Reformers and pietists were first applied to the Church of the Middle Ages, in time it was pushed further and further back: into the fourth century, into the post-apostolic period, and finally even into New Testament times, when the "Catholic" Luke is seen as opposed to the "Evangelical" Paul.

But this apostasy can be seen to be still earlier; in the Apostle Paul himself, as in John the Evangelist, there are two "layers": the one Paul is he, to use Luther's phrase, whom "Christ drives"; the other Paul thinks more magically-sacramentally or even more concretely-eschatologically, he is the more Catholic Paul. Once one drops this prejudice of an automatic decline of the Church in one way or another, the process by which Christ hands Himself on in a self-explaining tradition becomes manifest in the New Testament.

This does not, of course, appear obviously or immediately in all its compactness and logicality, but with patient and honest application, the student will discover it in this text and that. It affirms implicitly that the fundamental principle which the Roman Catholic Church unerringly teaches was operative in apostolic times, namely, the principle of the Church's everlasting identity with herself maintained by the help of the Holy Spirit. To express it in another way, this is the fundamental principle of the one and undivided tradition.

Yet more important is a second New Testament principle, the one which the Apostle John expresses so well and which all the other apostolic writers corroborate in their own way in many instances, i.e., that the Word was made flesh. This reality I began to see more and more clearly as the key to understanding everything Christian. And with it, we have all that is necessary for an understanding of the Roman Catholic Church.

From earliest times Christians have separated on this principle, and they do so still. Even the Evangelical Church acknowledges it in her theology, but that Church does not acknowledge all that it implies and hence does not draw the inevitable consequences. The Incarnation of the Word, according to St. John's Gospel, means its entry into the man Jesus, and hence also into the world of humanity which is His world. It is a penetration of the man Jesus and His world to the degree that He, the Eternal Word by whom all things were made and by whom all men are enlightened, now conceals Himself in the fleshly world of humanity. Thus Jesus reveals Himself as the Word in human history, so as to enable man to meet and experience His *doxa*—His life-illuminating reality. He does it in this and no other way, but in this way He does it fully and completely.

Hence, there is nothing "fleshly," nothing of the historical "substance" of the world, no secular organization that exists, which could not be a means, an instrument, a bearer, or a dwelling place of the power of the Word who has entered our world and our history. We see this in St. John's

Gospel itself, where we find not only the words of Jesus but also His works, signs, and wonders; not only His words and signs, but also His Body and Blood; not only His Body and Blood at one moment in history but throughout all time, and also His conveyance of Himself in the Holy Spirit; and not only Himself, but also His disciples and their disciples. The purpose of these is to make known and to propagate in the physical and temporal sphere, the Word's eternal claim, and with it the world's salvation, in various ways and in various senses. According to St. John's Gospel, revelation is fundamentally the penetration of all that belongs to the "flesh" by the Word. It is the operation of the Word through anything "fleshly" that He chooses for His purpose. It is for this reason that we find in this particularly "spiritual" gospel the very "material" or rather "fleshly" mediations of the Word. Some modern biblical scholars accept this by ascribing these accounts to a school of ecclesiastical editors who are supposed to have betrayed the spirituality of the original author. But with the above-mentioned utterances in St. John's Gospel, about the "fleshly" self-mediation of the Word, the very frequently mentioned "materialism" of the Roman Catholic Church is shown to be fundamentally apostolic.

The Word became "flesh" and not "word" (only spirit) as one might express it briefly, in opposition to a modern Evangelical interpretation of revelation—modern, but in inspiration probably quite like early Lutheranism. And as the Word became flesh and not simply word, there is now not only preaching but also sacraments; there is true dogma and not mere "affirmation"; but there is also sanctification and that change from glory to glory of which St. Paul speaks which is not merely the fulfillment of the existence of faith. There is finally the real indwelling of Christ in the Church, in her institutions, her laws, her liturgy, and in others things, too; and this is much more than mere momentary flashes in man's soul from the Scriptures.

The study of the New Testament gave me yet another insight. It is connected with the one already mentioned, but it concerns a particular aspect of the fact of Christ's Incarnation. It is the insight, if I may express it as untheologically as possible, that God has decided to save the world once and for all and in a very real manner. And the consequence of this, His deciding in our favor, is that the transient world in all its impermanence conceals within itself something of final value. God has decided in and with Jesus Christ, and He has decided for us. And now everything is determined by His resolve, by His decision. Having thus freely resolved, God has come to meet us, and this gracious condescension of His now stamps our whole world situation. As a result of God's resolve, time is different from what it was, and we see it as the time which is "fulfilled," and we have to live it, and can indeed truly live it. The fullness of time is no longer merely something to be realized in the future. We are not Hebrews, for whom God's time is only deferred and will be deferred while the present age lasts. It is no longer the period of the Old Covenant. We are Christians and as such we have to live in the Christian era, which in fact began with Christ's Resurrection. The future has already begun. Neither are we pagans whose future lies in the past; they have only an empty, hopeless void before them. The pagan period is no more. The calendar is no mere chance convention but a re-

flection of a real alteration in time. Because God has decided in our favor, the world, too, is other than it was. It is
one which, like the age, is filled with Christ; it is borne up,
permeated, and dominated by Him.

For this reason the Church, which takes in and absorbs
into herself this world of space and time is a temporal and
spatial embodiment. She is an "embodiment" in both an
active and a passive sense, for she is both that which makes
the space manifest and also its very body. This is what she is
as Christ's Body. As such she is the body of the new world;
the world sustained, permeated, and dominated by Christ.
Since God has decided in our favor, and since He, through
Christ, has remade the world, the Church is no longer something exceptional, peculiar, or foreign. Rather it is the world
that shuns Christ which is all these things. The Church, on
the other hand, is the norm, the truth, that which is native
to the world. The Church *is* the world now.

The Church *is* the world, but it is also a particular world.
It is only here that God's will, His full determination, becomes manifest. It is in the Body of Christ and within the
dimension of Gods' objective temple, His material city and
His real dwelling place, that the Church is most comprehensive and can be called the concrete aeon of God. God has
decided for a new world in the Church, and so all terrestrial
forms and structures will serve to achieve His purpose. From
this, according to the New Testament, stems the fact that
faith is based on concrete truths which demand concrete
manifestations of their reality. Thus, quite appropriately,
and in accordance with God's will for the world, the Church
makes decisions about her faith; she formulates it, defines it,

and overrides mere private judgments. Thus the fact that any uncertainty eventually comes to an end, an eschatological truth is already anticipated here on earth. Otherwise we should not be in the world about which God has decided. Revelation can attain to this concreteness, though not wholly and not continuously, but here and there, where it is most important. But this does not relieve the world or the believer of the need to think or study. It does, however, rid man of the illusions that truth can be found merely by thought or study or cannot be found at all.

Arising from God's will for the world and His purpose, is also the fact of the Church's authority. We see this in the New Testament in connection with the choice of apostles and disciples and the authorization and sending of those with special commissions; these bearers of commissions propagate themselves by the transmission of spiritual powers. The authorities so constituted make decisions for the Church in many matters, and in this way continue God's purpose or develop it. When certain decisions have to be made there is no invocation of the Spirit; the faithful are simply called upon to obey. Such decisions are those made by the apostles, or those which are made by proper authorities with the object of preserving the apostolic heritage. It is, therefore, by no means "biblical" to believe, as some Protestants do, that the Church can only be led by a council of the "brethren."

Right from the beginning, in New Testament times and afterward, the Church is led by a "hierarchy." This excludes neither those who have received charismatic gifts, nor the other members of the community, but it does not leave the final word with either. And this, too, is a subject for reflection and a matter of consequence for us in these latter days, for it does not mean that everything that is final must be postponed. It means the very contrary; that the contemporary can be final, even if hidden or veiled, as, for instance, in human decisions. In the New Testament, too, is the evident fact of undivided service in conjunction with asceticism. St. Paul is an example. As a rule it is not clearly seen that this undivided service of the Apostle Paul and the asceticism which goes with it, are means deliberately adopted to their end. In their nature, therefore, they represent an eschatological phenomenon. To what does all this talk of *eschaton*, all this eschatological awareness, amount, in consideration of this concrete, daily renewed anticipation of the future which is inherent in priestly celibacy and monasticism? It is in fact what may be called an eschatological existence. Here we see a concrete response, at least at one point, to Gods' decision, to God's resolve.

However, it would not be wise to emphasize these points too much, for their recognition is not ultimately a matter of New Testament interpretation, however much the New Testament may help in this matter. These things are often not enough seen because the student is possessed by a prejudice and a fear before attempting the interpretation, and these attitudes interfere at a critical moment with the process of interpretation. Even when such knowledge is gained by the study of the New Testament, people usually fail to draw the consequences. One has only to consider how much is admitted by Protestant exegetes and historians, and then to observe how it is rejected in practice, both dogmatically and ecclesiastically. That slanted judgment, or prejudice, which obstructs impartial interpretation is well expressed in relation to the familiar but misunderstood text of St. John's Gospel, "The spirit breathes where it will." According to those who think in this way, those words are supposed to mean that the Spirit of God, the pneuma, is not bound and can not be contained in texts, symbols, offices and institutions; not only because it does not need them, but also because, in them, it loses its freedom and is at the disposal of men. And those who are also possessed by fear go on to assert that such an attachment of the Spirit, and the power over it, claimed by man lead to an un-Christian feeling of security.

But we do not find even the seed of such a prejudice, such apprehensiveness in the New Testament. According to the New Testament the Spirit has quite definitely bound itself to texts and symbols in the sense that it makes use of these and no others, and these specifically in order to bring life and light to human beings. Finally, the actual text of the New Testament itself witnesses to this fact; but many deny it even though the Reformers themselves were still aware of it. In this document, people are familiar with spiritually inspiring hymns, which are unchanging, with spirit-created and spirit-engendering *homologesis* (confession) expressed in the texts; with the spirit bound up with water, for example, in order to bring about rebirth. That by such attachments the Spirit is limited and controlled does not seem to cause alarm in the New Testament. This would be true only if in all instances through such attachment (as, for example, in the symbols of bread and wine) automatic saving effects were possible and the spiritual response of obedience and faith were not required. The Spirit's attaching of itself to matter is but an intensification of its promised coming, its saving presence, and, therefore, of its (potential) saving effect. It is a proof of God's decisive offer, decided to the very letter or, to describe it differently, to the very "matter." It is never a separate spiritual or magical conveyance of salvation as the anti-Roman passion of the Enlightenment never gets tired of affirming. This passion continues to play a great part in the antisacramental utterances of well-known Protestant theologians. Because, for instance, the Spirit freely attaches itself to the water of baptism, we experience an expression of God's deliberate condescension; and because the power of its real effect is always "critical," in that it demands at least the eventual response of obedience, it does not promote *securitas* at all in the sense of human self-assurance. Yet it probably does encourage a certain confidence in God's offer of life, in the strength and mightiness of His intervention. It probably does give assurance of the urgency of His saving act, of the certainty of His resolve, and of the subsequent necessity of my decision.

This love of God for humanity, which stoops so far to meet us, condescending as the Risen Lord did in appearing to St. Thomas in the face of the faith of the other disciples, cannot but awaken a feeling of gratitude for God's simplicity which recognizes our human frailty, but it does not give "security." It even awakens, if you like, a certain "insecurity," i.e., the insecurity of one inescapably encompassed by God's loving kindness. The man who has experienced this knows that the Spirit and salvation meet him on quite a human, quite a commonplace, level; they meet him in such a manner that he cannot pretend he has not understood. Where then

is *securitas* basically possible? Of course, such profound condescension on the part of the God who has decided to save
us can be abused and is greatly abused, and undeniably, by
the faithful in the Roman Catholic Church, by *us*. But since
when has one judged a gift in terms of the danger of abuse?
In any case, who can set himself up as a judge in this matter?
Much that appears as self-assurance is simply that freedom
from restraint which is the good fortune of those who trust
God absolutely. Such people trust God because He puts
within our reach the means to save ourselves, i.e., His love,
with which indeed we can never catch up, but which is the
first and the last thing there is. And is it not true that much
that seems to be great self-distrust, even "fear and trem-
bling," much that seems to show a meek disquiet and cries
fervently "to God be the glory," is fundamentally nothing
less than self-assurance? In such cases, God is not allowed to
decide. He is obliged to leave everything in the balance, in
the balance not only of the concrete word of Holy Scripture,
but of the spiritual word which may possibly come forth
from the Scripture. This word of the Spirit never takes on
form, never becomes concrete; it never becomes outward and
objective, but is merely "picked up" at times in a sort of
existential faith, a faith, however, which by no means truly
exists because it vanishes as soon as it appears. Here everything remains uncertain, including the certitude of our uncertainty in the presence of the Self-revealing God. But does
this not amount in the end to a necessary erection of an absolute self-assurance?

I know that this idea of controlling God, and of the
human self-confidence lying behind it and encouraged by it,

can easily be seen to be fallacious, even by many in the Evangelical Church. I know, too, that this error which stems, appropriately enough, from Luther's theology of temptation, finds deeper roots in the frightful self-assurance of the late Medieval Church practice and its theological substructure. And from that source, a self-centered emotion has been abetted which can scarcely be eliminated even by instruction and knowledge. But whatever historical and psychological reasons there may be for this, we must affirm theologically and exegetically, if we accept the New Testament, that the Holy Spirit has clearly attached itself to the concrete means of salvation. It is therefore attached to the Church, together with her institutions, her offices, and the bearers of those offices. This attachment is to be understood as a fact which in no way weakens the power of the Spirit in all its varied manifestations, nor does it lessen its effect as an undivided connection with the eschatological character of our age—our historic period which has experienced the final and decisive condescension of God.

But something else must be mentioned, too. I think I have learned something from the New Testament which the Roman Catholic Church has taught infallibly from the very beginning. It is the simple fact that the Church comes before the individual Christian. And this "before" has not only a temporal but also a factual sense. She *is* Christ's Body, and is, in consequence, always more than the sum of its members and always "before" its members. She is indeed the Body of Jesus Christ who is the Head; the Body of the second, the final Adam. And just as we as human beings live from and in Adam, drawing from him that life which we pass on to succeeding generations, we, as baptized members of Christ's Body, drawing our spiritual life from Christ, must now imitate Him and bear His "image." As members of His Body, we draw our life from the Head, through His Body which is the Church.

The meaning of this is real and urgent. It means, to cite but one point, that we never receive the gift of life, the Spirit, except in and through the Church. The Spirit may speak to me with intensity in the isolation of subjectivity, although this occurs much more rarely than is imagined. Still more rarely, it may call a man to denounce a tired, unenthusiastic, and false mood which for the moment has been dominant in the Church. In any case, the Spirit usually calls within the Church. Proof lies in the fact that such a man is always calling on her behalf; he is a man calling *to* her, never *away* from her. This is especially true in the moment of the final painful conflict of one who is called upon to expose deep wounds and grave sins that have affected many in the Church. It is the Spirit in the Church which calls this man, too, and especially this man. It is the Spirit of Christ, the Holy Ghost, calling men, not to separate, but to subject themselves, not, of course, to the sins but to the Church. This is the way in which the Church is forever reforming herself. It is a reform from within, a reform which strengthens her. When the true Church reformer fails to gain his point, there is no other course open but to die giving his witness for the truth in the face of the spirit of falsehood which has overcome many of the members of the Church. If he leaves the Church, even inwardly (although this is when it matters), his apostasy does not remain inward; he puts his trust in his own pneuma, which may be quite genuine, rather than in the pneuma of the Church. He then resembles those spiritually gifted people of the Church of Corinth, who put their personal spiritual gifts in opposition to the doctrines of the apostles.

I do not wish to pass judgment here upon the character of Luther. But I want to state openly that his passionate piety seemed to be constantly and curiously permeated by a blind passion; and his polemics were not only conditioned by his times, as is often said. But they do not constitute a merely moral phenomenon, either. They are the polemics of an angry man for whom everything has gone wrong from the beginning; they show a man fighting for his life with half truths. I also do not wish to review here the reasons for the Reformation. There was no lack of reasons, at that time, when the Church was sick in head and members to a degree which we cannot imagine. But reasons for what sort of Reformation? Certainly not for the sort which leads to a schism in the Church, one which does violence to her nature and which is therefore valueless.

I will cite another example which shows the significance of the fact that the Church comes before the individual and this point is of particular interest to me. This is true in the interpretation of Holy Scripture which must be the responsibility of the Church and, in the long run, must be regulated by the Church. It must be in accord with the spirit of the Church and must ultimately be judged by the Church in regard to its truth. This does not mean that the interpreter is simply obliged to accept particular results of earlier exegetes, although such authors ought always to be respected. Nor does it mean that modern exegetes are obliged to accept exegetical methods which were once used and recognized in the Church, although one should, of course, bear in mind their value. Exegesis is in itself a historical and, therefore, a variable process. But because it is a historical process and truly alive, the fact must be realized that when it is practiced within the framework of the whole life of this world, exegesis must remain, and must move, in the milieu of the Spirit.

This Spirit is the Spirit as manifested both in the Bible and in the Church, and exegesis must permit itself to be bound by its power. But this has the additional implication that exegesis has to be achieved in the ideological sphere of the Church. This is so only because it is a function of that great and enduring interpretation which, in this period after Christ, must be practiced in the world of existence. It applies to everything in the Christian universe, of which even the anti-Christian outlook is a part. Only thus has it any claim upon our attention and only thus does it remain in the true spirit of Holy Scripture. Of course, the fact that I am a member of the Church does not mean that I necessarily interpret Holy Scripture correctly in any particular case. But I do know what the Church's claims are, and I am protected from the acceptance of a strange voice the more consciously I listen to the Church. The situation of the exegete with no dogmatic certitude who sits in isolation before a Bible, opened as it were for the first time, must be quite imaginary. Any exegete, without knowing or willing it, perhaps, is either conditioned by the Spirit of the Church or else stands in an ideological sphere foreign or even opposed to Holy Scripture. This is a situation which, looked at historically, indicates a breaking away from the life and ideas of the Church: it is an independent evolution. However, even from this position it is possible for a man to attain to the sphere of the true claims of Holy Scripture; and this is more likely if he is especially devoted to Holy Scripture, but it also can happen in unpredictable ways. Unfortunately, although it is usually the case that the obstacles in that strange or inimical sphere of life and thought are so great that a person remains fixed in that mental climate and fails to grasp the claims Scripture makes upon him. We are all to some extent in this situation, even those of us who live in and with the Church, or who, it might be better to say, leave her from time to time.

It is for this reason that we as exegetes must submit, in the final analysis, to the authority of the Church all the many real and unavoidable historical and exegetical problems of New Testament scholarship. Yet it must be remembered that these problems are posed by the total situation and are, therefore, not absolute. For some of modern existentialism, a product of the living conditions and ideological environment of a particular period, the statements of Holy Scripture about the Resurrection of Christ are of a merely mythological character. According to the Acts of the Apostles, they were also considered in this way by some of the ancient rationalists. Why? The usual reply is that the Resurrection would constitute a miracle and miracles are an offense to human reason, and even to human morality; although in more primitive times, when there was a more vital comprehension of the basic significance of myths, they were considered tolerable and even acceptable.

This view and this explanation of Christ's Resurrection are false. The report of it given in the New Testament is completely lacking in mythological characteristics. As there is nothing properly comparable with it in ancient religion and mythology, no parallel can be drawn. Moreover, the event is not recounted as a miracle. Rather it is recorded as a real historical event, *sui generis,* of unheard-of power and effect; and we have to content ourselves with this formal documentation. But why do people not grasp its meaning, at least in principle, as in general they do grasp or suspect the nature of Creation? Because people in general and their methods of thinking, have shifted away from the sphere of life and immediacy of the Spirit; the sphere which the event of Christ's Resurrection created, and which existed along with the faith of the first eyewitnesses. This is the sphere of life and ideas which is still the Church's sphere. Indeed, it has been the Church's claim from the beginning to be able to deal with man and his interpretation of existence, on religious, moral, and intellectual levels.

But I have another and final point of view from which I would like to speak. It is one which motivates me in my endeavor to clarify the reasons, developing from New Testament research, which brought about my conversion. Year by year, my conviction grew that, according to the New Testament, there is but one Church, one single Church. I saw that the Church's unity is a quality which is essential to her, and that her unity must be seen as the concrete, historical unity of her fundamental aspects; unity in her means of salvation, her faith, her offices, her law, and, of course, among her members.

Let us for one moment turn our gaze away from everything else. No one can deny that the unity of the Church is
implied in the very notion of the People of God, the New
Israel, or the Body of Christ. But this unity is based on the
fact that the Church of the New Testament is nothing less
than the earthly and heavenly concretion of God's loving-
kindness for the whole world, of that unifying motion of His
love which desires all that exists. Love is harmony. Harmony
is achieved from within, but, owing to its nature, it cannot
remain inside. It penetrates into the world outside and so
gains access to all the elements of which the Church is made.
Of course, harmony is fulfilled only in God's future, but this
future was already present to the world in the Incarnation
of the Word and in the Resurrection of Jesus Christ—in the
Church, to be exact. Harmony is already achieved in concrete terms, in the present, because Christ's Body on the
cross united Jews and pagans and propitiated God, in the
Church; the Church which was concealed in that Body and
which was formed from it by the Holy Ghost. No one can
quote any biblical passage which states that the unifying
Church is merely that existing in the hearts of true Christians living everywhere in the world. And no one can prove
from Scripture that the Church's unity is like that of branches
which join in the tree, in which each of the branch Churches
makes a contribution to some higher, invisible unity. Isn't
this image rather in the category of a "pathetic fallacy"; visible branches joined to an invisible tree? And finally, no one
can prove from Scripture that the Church's unity is merely
an eschatological unity to be achieved only on the Last Day,

and that, because of this, all Churches (really all?) are tending to progress ultimately toward the One Church.

As we know, the field (to use a biblical image) is not sown on the Last Day; then it is that the wheat and the tares are separated. It is not then that the net is cast for the first time, but then that the bad fish are separated from the good. How could Jesus have prayed for the unity of His disciples, implying that their disunity would cause the world to disbelieve, if what He had in mind was only a future unity? Is it not more likely that He was thinking of a present unity which concretely and from the beginning anticipated the future? In the Evangelical Churches of divided Christendom it has been known for a long time that a concrete and present unity was intended. So long as these Churches were orthodox, as the Greek Orthodox Church is to this day, they claimed, at least in practice, that they constituted the only true Church. They held at the same time that their opponent, the Roman Catholic Church, was the antichrist. But the ecumenical strivings of contemporary Protestants prove that the consciousness of a concrete and present unity is still alive. Many of the champions of the ecumenical movement feel this unity to be necessary, not only for practical ecclesiastical or religio-political reasons but also because the seventeenth chapter of St. John's Gospel carries some weight with them. Of course, the movement in question reveals by its theoretical principles and its practical behavior that it is not unbiased in its attitude to the nature of a harmonizing unity. It weakens before the idea of a centralized authority that would be necessary to achieve this unity, and goes as far as "squaring the circle." The world suffers as a result of this and will go on suffering, for its own unity will not be achieved if Christendom is divided. The sole harmonizing power of unity, that concrete movement of the unifying power of God, is obstructed within and without. The nations achieve no earthly state of peace; all they achieve is tenuous armistice. And the signs multiply that the only way they will unite is in a unity of hatred.

What I have mentioned are only a few of the insights I have gained in the course of the years and through my studies in the interpretation of the New Testament. On the one hand, my research was prepared for by many practical experiences; on the other, it was corroborated by such experiences. These insights would not permit me to remain outside the fold of the Roman Catholic Church, which is, of her nature, one—*the* one. She is always *more* than the sum of her members; she is, therefore, *above* each individual member. In her, and through her, God demonstrates that He has entered into time to meet us; He demonstrates His will which He made manifest in the Incarnation of His logos. In the Church and through her, as time passes, our Lord unfolds His fullness, the fullness of truth, and He continues to give Himself in loving-kindness to men for their salvation.

Of course, these insights were not handed to me "ready-made," bidding me simply to draw the consequence. They developed for me gradually, through my constant appraisal of the New Testament and under the influence of many events and meetings with various people. They furnished me with reasons so powerful that I felt myself impelled and commanded—after great hesitation, but at length with decision and joy—to go off into that strange land in which my real home seemed to lie. There, if God so wills it, I shall at last feel completely at home.

May God reward those who stood by me at my leave-taking!

Index

A NOTE ON THE TYPE

IN WHICH THIS BOOK IS SET

This book is set in Baskerville, a Linotype face, created from the original types used by John Baskerville, the eighteenth-century typefounder and printer. This type has long been considered one of the finest book types ever developed. The letters are wide and open and have a businesslike approach. The finer hairlines give exquisite delicacy. The heavier strokes give color and strength. The relation of the two in combination gives a brilliant effect and makes for easy reading. The book was composed and printed by the Wickersham Printing Company of Lancaster, Pa., and bound by Moore and Company of Baltimore. The typography and design are by Howard N. King.